THE URBAN EDGE

D0770299

The Urban Edge

Where the City Meets the Sea

Editors: Joseph E. Petrillo
Peter Grenell

Published by The California State
Coastal Conservancy in cooperation
with William Kaufmann, Inc.,
Los Altos, California

Editors: Joseph E. Petrillo and Peter Grenell
Managing Editors: Pat Murphy and Dewey Schwartzenburg
Copy Editor: Nathan Salant
Book and Cover Design: Thomas Ingalls and Gail Grant
Photo Research: Monica Suder
Editorial Assistance: Scott McCreary

Cover Photo Credits:

Front, top to bottom: Richard Sexton, Dan Esgro,
                          Fred E. Basten, and Charles W. Moore
Back, top to bottom: Liza Riddle and DeWitt Jones

This project is supported by a grant from the
National Endowment for the Arts in Washington, D.C.,
a federal agency.

William Kaufmann, Inc.
95 First Street
Los Altos, CA 94022

Library of Congress Cataloging in Publication Data

Main entry under title:

The Urban edge.

  Bibliography: p.
  Includes index.
  1. Coastal zone management—California—
Addresses, essays, lectures.   2. Waterfronts—
California—Planning—Addresses, essays, lectures.
3. Waterfronts—California—Planning—Costs—
Addresses, essays, lectures.   I. Petrillo, Joseph E.
II. Grenell, Peter.   III. California State Coastal
Conservancy.
HT393.C3U73 1984   333.91'7'09794   84-29265
ISBN 0-86576-078-0 (pbk.)

CONTENTS

"... The primeval meeting place of the elements of earth and water, a place of compromise and conflict and eternal change."
— Rachel Carson[1]

"For the gifts of life are the earth's and they are given to all, and they are the songs of birds at daybreak, Orion and the Bear, and dawn seen over ocean from the beach."
— Henry Beston[2]

Introduction

The interactions which occur across boundaries—such as cell membranes, the earth's crust and the atmosphere, edges of urban settlements, and the coastline—are extremely complex, full of ambiguity, and profound. The life force is more directly apprehensible "on the edge," especially at the meeting of land and sea.

Regrettably, where people have settled on the coast, habitations, work places, and leisure places have too often ignored these fundamental aspects of the coastal environment. The result has been architecture and urban development that all too frequently have not harmonized with their unique surroundings; that were, in the jargon, "environmentally unsound." The visual clutter and ecological insensitivity that characterize much development along the California coast reflect a barrenness of outlook that is basically inimical to life. Characterized by incongruity with site and surroundings, bad coastal design reflects a lack of harmony with self and with others, and represents a movement toward disorganization, toward the chaos of entropy.

Of particular concern are the urban edges, where California's cities meet the sea. Over two-thirds of the state's population resides in two coastal urban centers: the San Francisco Bay Area and the Los Angeles Basin. In these and other coastal urban areas, the competition for waterfront space and the need for public access to the shore exacerbate the problems of past haphazard development and present deterioration. The problems of the urban waterfront are matched by its potential—in the urban coastal environment, the varied physical context and multiplicity of needs make design a challenge and an opportunity. In contrast, design for undeveloped rural areas on the coast, such as Big Sur or Mendocino County, must take into account fewer but more obvious considerations, such as the impact of development on views, sensitive habitats, landforms, and traffic circulation.

For the past thirteen years, the State of California has regulated design and development in the coastal zone, a band of land that stretches from Oregon to Mexico and extends from a few city blocks inland to as much as five miles from the shore. In 1972, California's voters approved a citizen-initiated referendum, Proposition 20, intended to protect the state's coastal resources. In 1976, Proposition 20 led to the adoption by the Legislature of a program for the protection and enhancement of the California coast. The creation of an agency to plan and regulate coastal development, the Coastal Commission, and one to restore coastal resources, the Coastal Conservancy, were the two most prominent parts of that program. In 1981 the Legislature expanded that program by adopting the "Urban Waterfront Act of 1981" and authorizing the State Coastal Conservancy to undertake and fund restoration of the state's urban waterfronts and "to promote excellence of design and [to] . . . stimulate projects which exhibit innovation in sensitively integrating man-made features into the natural coastal environment." In 1983 the Legislature further confirmed the state's commitment to waterfront restoration by authorizing the sale of $650 million in bonds to fund the program.

California's coastal program has attempted to encourage and, where necessary, require designs which take into account a proposed development's immediate and surrounding environmental characteristics. Too often, designers of coastal projects have concentrated almost exclusively on the structures themselves and their component parts, and have not given adequate thought to protection of scenic values, ecologically sensitive areas, and public access to the shoreline. The Coastal Commission has tried, therefore, to provide design parameters, an "envelope" based on the Coastal Act within which the structure must fit.

But what of the designer, the interpreter and articulator of society's will in wood and concrete? Caught between client demands for "maximum leasable area," a multitude of regulatory requirements, site constraints, antagonistic community residents, and personal needs for a feeling of achievement, the designer may feel limited to few options, none truly satisfying.

John Burchard, Dean of MIT's School of Humanities and Social Studies, has commented upon the "widening rings of visual disorder" in our urban environments and has urged us to recapture our sensitivity to nature. In considering the role of the artist and the architect in this endeavor, he notes that: "The power of the artist and the architect will never be there until it rests on a large and positive support from a citizenry which has learned *to see*."[3] Thus, the designer, the client, and the public all must learn *to see* the coast for what it is and to understand their ancient and intimate connections to it.

Finally, although many examples of good waterfront design are given in this book, one must distinguish design viewed from a distance from that enjoyed from within. In the final analysis, one cannot overemphasize the value of accessibility by the general public and the sensitivity to their enjoyment as the chief component of the waterfront experience. Places to gather and stroll near the water's edge, with comfortable places to sit and rest or to eat and drink, are almost all that is needed. These few simple elements can raise the design of an urban waterfront from merely a collection of structures to a place of enjoyment.

A few basic themes form the heart of this book, setting it apart, we hope, from the many critiques of architectural designs of one sort or another, and the many other volumes glorifying the beauties of or decrying the destruction of the coast. The writers—including a practicing designer, scholars of architecture, public servants, and economists—review the historic and present contexts of coastal design with particular reference to California's urban coast (Part I); describe some significant attempts to generate environmentally compatible design through regulation, publicly initiated development, and direct community involvement (Part II); and discuss the economic advantages of compatible coastal design and various ways to bring good design within economic reach (Part III).

The State Coastal Conservancy, co-publisher of this book, is a State agency established by legislation in 1976. The Conservancy is charged with protecting, preserving, and restoring coastal resources through programs of land acquisition, waterfront restoration, wetland enhancement, public access, agricultural preservation, open space protection, and aid to local land trusts. The agency works with local governments, nonprofit organizations, citizens' groups, and other public agencies. The Conservancy was formed chiefly to resolve coastal land use conflicts which are not readily amenable to regulation and to help coastal communities implement publicly beneficial coastal development projects. In urban areas, these focus on increasing public access, shoreline amenities, and marine-oriented activities consistent with protection of sensitive habitat, open space, and scenic areas.

Observation of the Coastal Commission's experiences since 1976 and reflection on the Conservancy's own, more recent experience led Conservancy staff members to the conviction that a document designed to educate the public about basic coastal design issues is needed. Hence, this book.

Notes:

1. Rachel Carson, *The Edge of the Sea* (Boston: Houghton Mifflin Company, Signet Books, 1955) p. vii.

2. Henry Beston, *The Outermost House* (New York: The Viking Press, 1956) p. 222.

3. John Burchard, "Forward to Gyorgy Kepes," *The New Landscape in Art and Science* (Chicago: Paul Theobald and Company, 1956) p. 15.

Section One
Overview: A Look
at the Urban Waterfront

What makes coastal development good, bad, or indifferent? Some say that this judgment is purely subjective, based on personal preferences.

Regulation of coastal development in California has implied otherwise. According to the California Coastal Act of 1976, new urban development on the coast must be compatible with the character and scale of surrounding areas. In scenic areas, new development must be subordinate to the character of its setting.

The California Coastal Commission, the state agency charged with approving development along the coast, does not consider a structure's design in isolation. The agency is primarily concerned with the suitability of the design for the environment —a view of architecture that seems more in keeping with the oriental tradition of seeking harmony with nature than with the western tradition of imposing a human type of order upon the natural world. In the western tradition, architects create a design by arranging a set of design elements to harmonize with each other, though not always with their natural setting.

In its review of a project, the Coastal Commission considers a number of other requirements; these are described in the discussion of regulation found in the second section of this book. But the suitability of a design for its coastal environment is clearly a prime consideration in the Commission's review.

The two essays in this section provide an overview of urban waterfront design— on the California coast and elsewhere. These essays—by architect Charles W. Moore and historian David Gebhard—reveal that the Coastal Commission is not alone in emphasizing compatibility of structure and environment as an indicator of good design. Moore describes memorable coastal cities. Each one, he says, is an example of how citizens have shaped their city "to liberate the individual genius or potential of each particular site." Gebhard has taken the notion of suitability for the coast a step further in describing the history of California coastal design. The designs he discusses have been shaped by the idea of what the coast symbolized, more than by the physical facts of hills, beach, surf, and ocean. His review of California's history describes the consequences of different views of the coast.

The Edges of the World:
An International Tour by the Shore

CHARLES W. MOORE

Though the surface of our planet is mostly water, the seas and lakes and rivers remain mysterious and fascinating. People from the inland flock to the shore to be as close as possible to the excitement along this edge where water and land collide. They come for the exhilaration of what was once described as a "mental leaning out over," a sensation which is invoked by a few well-conceived places and heightened by proximity to the enigmatic vastness of even small bodies of water.

Alas, during the last two centuries, as more people are finding more ways to delight in the shoreline, more and more of it has been taken away from them. Use of the shoreline has been usurped by giant ports and altogether extraneous uses, such as warehouses and factories—far more than require a proximity to ships or water. We have begun, a little, to recognize the attraction and the attractiveness of the land's edges and have made some effort to preserve what is left. We have passed laws restricting what can be built near the water, but now find ourselves in danger of so confining the possibilities that we wipe out the magic we sought to regain.

Those places along the shore that people will travel halfway around the world to visit usually present a dazzling variety of uses and shapes, often intricately composed. As part of this colorful mixture, they all share that quality of a "mental leaning out over." Shorelines restricted to a single use or just a few uses are often dreary disappointments.

The world presents an exciting array of seashores that could serve as models—not as limits—for our own. It is the purpose of this essay to describe some of them, to see what they have in common, and note how widely they differ. From the hundreds of places along the shore that I have sought out or stumbled upon, I have selected here the most memorable. They are all special places, with separate identities that cause them to remain in the memory. What most of them share is that they were made, or at least completed, with human hands. The most enticing places along the shore invariably give evidence of human occupation. The places I have listed were all occupied and shaped by human beings, with a great deal of care and love and an unrestrained enthusiasm to liberate the individual genius or potential within each particular site.

The places fall into six groups, depending on the nature of the shore they occupy: in the first form, lands project into the water in headlands, promontories, points, or peninsulas; in the second, the sea penetrates the land in bays, harbors, fjords, or inlets; in the third, bluffs or cliffs tower above the sea along a relatively straight section of coast; in the fourth, the land slopes gently toward the sea with a beach, a marsh, a greenward, or an esplanade at the boundary; in the fifth, a river comes from inland to mingle its waters with the ocean; in the sixth, an island or a whole archipelago rises from the sea. Memorable places, it is worth noting, can be found in all six configurations, but they are always distinguishable from what lies beside or around them: you know when you have arrived, and when you have left.

Headlands, Promontories, Points, and Peninsulas–Positions of Prominence and Power

A lighthouse flashing at the end of a point, a lonely house perched on a crag, a city that towers over the sea on a finger of land—these are images that linger in the memory. Where man's structures extend into the water on fingers of land or artificial constructions, they can leave a vivid, singular image.

MICHAEL E. BRY

The impact of man on the shoreline ranges from the lonely isolation of the solitary lighthouse to the crystalline towers of the modern city. At right, the lighthouse at Pidgeon Point rises from a barren, rocky coast, while at left, the man-made structures of San Francisco crowd together down to the very edge of the waters of San Francisco Bay.

San Francisco can be seen across the water as a single, but miraculously complex, picturesque vision. Like Istanbul—with its great domes, Ottoman churches, and slender minarets—the city rises to be visible all at once. Smaller cities—Ibiza in the Balearic Islands off Spain, and Split on the Dalmatian coast of Yugoslavia—rise from heavy, ancient fortress walls to tower above the water, dramatic symbols of strength and power. In Villefranche-sur-Mer, a picturesque hilltown on the French coast, the shapes of buildings, packed tightly together on the slope, accentuate the hill and fit into the landscape even more naturally than the natural landscape itself. A look at towns like these makes the designer of coastal places aware that he can do better to increase the prominence and splendor of nature than to cringe in the face of something already wonderful. Adding only the unconvinced and unconvincing diminishes and smudges the form of the land, rather than adding to its power.

A city on a peninsula need not tower over its surroundings to be a memorable place. Charleston, South Carolina is a middle-size city on a low-lying narrow strip of land bounded by two rivers which flow just beyond their confluence into the Atlantic. Although Charleston is on the coast, the summers are long and hot and still. Because land was constricted, the designers of the city had to invent a house form that fit into small quarters but still allowed the breezes to pass through. They devised something called the "single house," a string of rooms on perhaps three floors which are perpendicular to the street with a veranda passing along the front of all the rooms and then onto a garden. Air passes through the rooms and the veranda and the garden and makes life a little more bearable in the sultry summers. The result of this tight packing that still allowed room for air to move is a city of considerable urbanity with a sense of specialness, distinct from the open countryside around it. The suburbs, which now stretch in many directions from the city, have none of this special sense and do not fit the land with the same sensitivity as Charleston. One of the most singular places in Charleston is the Battery, a park at the tip of the peninsula where a sea wall, with a view out over the open water, is positioned three or four feet above the street and the cars. There is a feeling that this wall is independent of both the cars and the water, marking vividly the edge of something special, so that to walk along it is to "lean out over."

Occasionally on this planet, there is a massive outcropping at the edge of the sea, a rock like Gibraltar or Calpe in Spain, or even Morro Rock on the coast of California, where any amount of building remains much less important and almost invisible in the face of the great upthrust of stone. In the two

CHARLES MOORE

Spanish examples, the streets and buildings of sizable human settlements cling to the lower edges of these huge slabs.

A much more delicate intervention, although still bold, is the Walker house that Frank Lloyd Wright designed at the end of the Carmel beach in California. This beach is wide and sandy and has, where it ends, the first of a set of small outcroppings which extend from the mainland into the ocean. Wright designed for this first small crag a low-lying house with its eaves outspread on a hexagonal honeycomb of a plan, which makes obtuse angles that fit smoothly and naturally with the rock on which they perch. The living room occupies the end of the point, with glass all around and a walled terrace which makes the delicate structure comfortable in the teeth of the sea. Thus, the house becomes an extension of the rock, which is, for all its tininess, sufficiently dense and powerful to face the waves.

One last category of headlands or points is the man-made version, the pier which projects into the sea from beaches and headlands across the world. Something about the actual, physical invasion of the sea's territory seems to bring out an exhilaration, a sense of celebration. Piers everywhere are places where people go for relaxation and enjoyment—from Brighton pier in England, to the pier in Santa Monica. Sometimes these amusements have to do with fishing or the things one actually does on the sea; sometimes the excitement of the ocean crashing below and the thrill of being perched out above the waves is enough.

The Walker House in Carmel (above), designed by Frank Lloyd Wright, is an example of successful integration of design and nature. The house seems to rise organically out of the rocky crag on which it is built.

A great upthrust of stone at the edge of the sea, such as Morro Rock in Morro Bay (opposite), dominates and gives definition to its site. Man-made structures are dwarfed by such massive outcroppings.

Bays, Harbors, Inlets–The Sheltered Shore

In the protective embrace of a curve of land, human settlements can be sheltered from the fury of the storm, yet share in the mysterious magic of the meeting of land and water. These settlements range in size from great cities to only a few houses. Some of the bays are hardly bays at all and great cities sweep around the crescent of their shores. At night, these great arcs of urbanity around a bay can present glittering spectacles of light: Santa Monica, for instance, as it is seen from Malibu, or the Malabar coast of Bombay.

Perhaps the most exciting spectacle of all is Rio de Janeiro. Great pinnacles of rock rise along the multiple curves of bay sheltered from the ocean by wide, bright white beaches. There is not a simple mound of buildings here, but rather a complex arena of bays and harbors and valleys and uplands around the feet of the upthrust mountains. High buildings have climbed all over everything and have gathered thickly at the beach at Copacabana and in pockets of downtown to make little mountains of their own in an extension of this magic landscape.

On the Amalfi coast of Italy, numbers of towns pile almost vertically onto the cliffs, usually where a bay or an indentation in the land makes a giant amphitheater. The steps of the amphitheater are jumbles of multicolored buildings, each with a view back out to the center of town and the sea. Amalfi, Positano, and Capri are probably the most famous Italian towns in this category. On the Dalmatian coast of Yugoslavia, the drama is of slightly smaller scale, but just as intense, with towns crowding the edges of bays which bring the water into the heart of the city.

Perhaps the most perfect of all, on the northern Italian coast, is Portofino, where multi-storied buildings press tight to the sea around a little harbor extended by rocks and a breakwater. A piazza at the head of the harbor, with tables and chairs and umbrellas, has a paved floor which slips down under the water so that boats can pull up beside the tables. It is as though the whole center of the city, the stage for the amphitheater of buildings which surrounds it, is somehow subject to the forces of the deep as it extends from the comfortable life on land directly down under the water, a fitting set for the actions of Endymion.

Bluffs, Cliffs–The Dramatic Edge

Where the coastline is straight but rugged, high bluffs or cliffs rising dramatically above the edge of the water provide coastal aeries, where human intervention has happened with success. On our continent, perhaps the most dramatic city high above the water is Quebec, on the St. Lawrence River. Quebec has a lower city next to the seaway, then cliffs, then an upper city high above. In the upper city is a great hotel, the Chateau Frontenac, with a wide terrace several hundred feet long called the Terrasse Dufferin. From here, the splendid sense of windswept advantage makes an extraordinarily memorable place. The edge of this great terrace, as in any such high place, is the key. One can stand with the great copper roofs of the hotel behind, with promenades all around. Just beyond the railing, the drop to the lower town and the river creates an edge where physical, even mental "leaning out over" is a thrill.

High above the Amalfi coast, Ravello is a tiny city with a situation similar to the Dufferin terrace, with a remarkable garden at that key position. Along the very edge of the garden is a walk with a marble rail whose palisades support busts of important people, all arranged in a kind of giddy jeopardy with the sky and—1,500 feet below—the Mediterranean. Taormina, farther south in Sicily, is a village with a long past and a vivid outlook. There, a Roman amphitheater village occupies the terrace position with the view of the sea far below. In all three—Quebec, Ravello, and Taormina—the drama starts with an enormous vertical distance from sea to occupied territory. But in each case, the hand of man has dramatized the edge, the belvedere, the place where one can stand or sit and survey what seems to be half the world.

Sometimes the exciting edge is at the top of a much shorter dimension. The bluffs near Tunis provide a site for the residential and resort suburb of Sidi bou Said, where the picturesque, small-scale buildings of this elegant and ancient village stop, with sudden drama, at the edge of a cliff with the Mediterranean far below. Here, the excitement comes from highly choreographed surprises, where the tiny spaces in between the white walls suddenly give way to the wide open surface of the sea and sky.

The village of Clovelly, on the north Devon coast of England, reverses that choreography. It is disposed along a single street, which goes from the top of the bluff down, very steeply, on steps and switchbacks and every other means available, to the water's edge. The town's excitement comes not from a particular view of the water or even a continuing view of the water, but from an unfolding in which that view is caught and then obscured and then seen in another light, perhaps at the end of the tunnel of a narrow street or from a belvedere as the street comes to the edge and turns.

Savannah, Georgia is a city laid out on a high bluff which overlooks the Savannah River and the sea. The bluff comes to an abrupt end with a steep drop to the edge of the water. On the shore below, a long warehouse building, Factor's Walk, bridges the vertical distance from shoreline to bluff. This building served as a warehouse for the goods coming into the port and linked the activities at the bottom with its upper stories by means of an extraordinarily elaborate system of ramps and bridges to the side of the bluff and to its top. The building obscures much of the view of the water from the edge of the bluff, but substitutes an astonishingly rousing, three-dimensional world of ramps and bridges, and affords, from the spaces in between and from the upper floors of the buildings themselves, a richly complex view of the river flowing into the sea.

The human intervention in these places on bluffs and cliffs has provided a dramatization of the view. In places like Factor's Walk, the sense of human movement and the excitement of the port have intensified the drama. Again, the message seems to be that a wide variety of human acts is acceptable and even admirable if those acts are themselves imaginative and sensitive to the site.

Beaches—A Gentle Meetingplace

At other places where the coast is straight, the meeting between land and water is much more gentle. Beaches or greenswards slide down to the surface of the water and leave the drama to the waves, which come rolling in over the sand or splash at the feet of green slopes.

The beach at California's Carmel is a particularly popular and beautiful stretch of waves and sand with a street weaving in and out of cypress and other trees and houses along the edge. The white sands of Miami Beach, Florida provide a foreground for a set of skyscraper hotels which allow the many visitors a view of the ocean. The tall buildings themselves, in a long line along the coast, form a memorable background, a man-made cliff edge to the wide sand and the sea. The Chicago waterfront provides even larger towers spaced along its long beach, the real front of the city, with wide parks between the towers and the sand. Layers of boulevards stretch through the parks. We've been taught that the presence

Ravello, on the Amalfi Coast of Italy, is a tiny city built on the steep slopes below a great cliff. In such a place, awareness of the sea is pervasive.

CHARLES MOORE

Mont St. Michel, rising out of the shallow waters off the coast of Brittany, is a single dramatic island enhanced by the human structures surmounting it.

In Clovelly, on the north Devon coast of England, the walk down to the sea is full of continuous surprises as the sea is seen, then lost, then found again.

The Urban Edge

In San Francisco, over the last century and more, the plunge from land to water at the beach has been celebrated by a single building which leans out over the cliff edge of the city's western boundary. The famous Cliff House is seen here in four of its varied incarnations.

The Urban Edge

of automobiles at the front door of cities or right next to the water is in some way offensive, but for many in Chicago, the pleasures of the daily drive along the waterfront could not be achieved in a more effective way. The seafront promenades in smaller cities—such as Nice and Cannes—combine automobile traffic and opportunities to sit in the sun along the beach or on the terraces of grand hotels.

A simple, continuous face of buildings can make a civilized, even monumental, edge to the sea. In Helsinki, Finland a government center faces the port beside a long boulevard. On the land side, there stands a range of elegantly spare, classical buildings, all about the same height. A gap between them leads to a square just off the harbor, where the national cathedral rises in domes and spires behind the flat seafront. This capital city shows a civilized facade to the world, a powerful expression of its importance.

Along the coast of New England, there are small towns where an opposite, but also memorable, arrival of land at the seaside occurs. In Castine, Maine, for instance, or in Little Compton, Rhode Island, fields that look as though they might be at home somewhere far inland on a farm appear at the very edge of the deep. Their insouciance and the emergence of this fertile land at such a magic edge with hardly a whisper ingrain a powerful and lasting image.

One of the most enduring images of the sea and of its edge involves engulfment—in some way going under it. Poetic images of Endymion or the engulfed cathedral of Debussy's music evoke a mysterious, even frightening, vision of sliding under the waves. This image is given architectural form at the foot of the main boulevard of Lisbon. A paved square meets the edge of the water and the steps of a landing disappear beneath the surface, inviting descent into the deep, or, more usefully, a place to step onto a little boat. On the Mediterranean coast near Genoa, the immersion image is the basis for a giant statue of Christ in a deep bay right at the shore. You look down into the waters of a lost world and find there the familiar form of Jesus.

Rivers, Inlets—By the Running Water

From the beginnings of human settlement, the places where rivers come into the sea and make a water link between inland towns and distant ports have invited occupancy. The Moroccan city of Rabat is located on flat land on both sides of a little valley where a river flows into the ocean: the older city on one side, the new city on the other. On a much smaller scale, Jenner, on the California coast where the Russian River comes into the sea, occupies a place so special that its tiny, often flimsy houses seem protected by the grandeur of the site. For all the transience and the crowding together of little buildings, the town remains memorable.

A grander, more singular town, where a river comes into a sea with great differences in tide, is Portmeirion, on the Welsh coast. The town is a synthetic village of houses brought from all corners of England, the lifelong dream of Sir Clough Williams-Ellis, who established here a tourist delight made of bits and snippets of the inland landscape. Portmeirion sits tightly on the edge of a river which becomes, at low tide, a vast and mysterious sea of sand.

A number of very attractive towns of every possible size occur where an inlet links the sea on one side with a little basin for boats then continues farther inland to a bigger lake. Charlevoix, Michigan is such a place, though the big water is Lake Michigan and not the sea. The city is a composition in three scales, with the big lake, a little basin and an inland lake all hooked together by a channel, with spaces for all kinds of water pleasures.

Farther inland, rivers make an important connection in our minds with the mysteries of the deep. Herman Melville wrote glowingly of the attractiveness of little bodies of water running down to the sea and carrying the human imagination with them. It is extraordinary how effectively water in a city or a village releases the claustrophobia of its landlocked environs by setting our minds free to follow its course down to the vastness of the sea. Lower Slaughter, in the Cotswolds in the west of England, is a tiny and very pretty village built along an open space through which a little river runs. The sense of that village would be far different if an asphalt road ran where the river runs. The stream does what the road could never do, beckoning us to follow it down to the ocean.

Cambridge, in England, arranged along the Cam and the Granta rivers, presents a splendid spectacle of colleges whose so-called Backs—really, their green-lawned fronts—form a gorgeous chain of open spaces along the water. Revelers in punts, long boats propelled by poles to the bottom, ply the stream and enjoy the sequence of open spaces. Again, these colleges are very different, one from another, going from buildings tight against the river to walls with greenswards behind to grassy banks. Once more, a composition, a sequence of events with the recurrence of familiar motifs and then the introduction of surprises, makes the passage a fascinating one.

Perhaps the most popular riverfront in North America is the tiny one of the San Antonio River in downtown San Antonio, saved 50 years ago from being covered over as a mere drainage ditch. It now is an attraction that is beloved of San Antonians and draws millions of tourists each year to enjoy the sidewalk cafes, the fountains, the shops, the restored buildings and the long walks along the banks of this stream, which is only about 25 feet wide. Visitors can also ride on the river and delight in the shoreline drama from boats, which serve as moving vantage points and restaurants. Here, particularly, the pleasure is in surprise and change and an elaborate and fascinating choreography along the water's edge.

Islands—Places of Mystery and Magic

Our last category, perhaps the most special of all, is islands: single islands, paired, or whole archipelagos. In these magic places the human presence is fragile, tenuous, and still wondrous as we pit our own existence and works against the powerful and mysterious sea.

There are, of course, whole cities built on archipelagos with canals for streets: Venice, Bangkok, Amsterdam, and others. A look at Venice raises a question: Why isn't this urban model, based on water and so wonderfully successful and enjoyable on the Venetian lagoons and canals, one of the models for cities that might be used everywhere? The wonders of Venice are too extensive to elaborate here; John Ruskin and others have written many books about the water and these remarkable creations of humankind on the land. It is worth noting that the canals range in size from tiny channels only one boat wide to the Grand Canal, which, on its sinuous loop through the archipelago, provides maximum frontage along its banks. This wide canal turns into even larger lagoons, where architectural wonders can sparkle on islands far out across the waters.

Another breed of islands is the single peak rising off the shore or on the distant sea, enhanced sometimes by human works. Mont Saint Michel, in the tidal quicksands off the coast of Brittany, is among the most celebrated of such places, a little peak of an island with the village wrapped around its lower slopes and a splendid, spired religious edifice crowning the top.

There are larger islands where the image is of green fields and separate buildings. California's special island, Santa Catalina, 25 miles off the coast of Long Beach, has always been a magic land. When the Spaniards landed, they discovered a group of people that were taller, fairer and more advanced in the civilized arts than their counterparts on the mainland. Hundreds of years later, there is still a magic to Catalina for the tourists and merrymakers who take the boat or planes to this mystical place. One of the great physical successes of Catalina is that human habitation, which has been kept close beside the little harbor at Avalon, has been allowed to touch and even extend over the sea but has been kept away from the fields and grassy headlands which sur-

round it. Thus, a configuration similar to the villages along the Mediterranean's edge is achieved with a town which is tied to the sea, in surprising and delightful contrast to the surrounding open fields.

It is no accident that some islands have been marked as holy. There is a holy isle off the west coast of Scotland and another one off the east coast of England. Access to the eastern one, Lindisfarne, can be gained only at low tide; when the tide is high, the island is alone. On this island, a castle rises high above the sea. It was remodeled by Sir Edwin Lutyens into a house of great warmth, sheltered by the hard stone walls against the ocean's ravages. The western island, Holy Isle, named because Christian conversion came from the Irish coast to this place, seems very tiny, vulnerable, and far away—a place for magic.

The last island, different from all the rest, but carrying the message father, is Bedloe's Island in New York harbor, from which the Statue of Liberty rises. Here a single work, a big piece of sculpture, has stood for a century as a beacon, an announcement of the freedoms and the opportunities of the New World.

The Value of Variety

Here, then, is a sampling of places along the shores of the world which stick in the memory. They come in all configurations, located on headlands, bays, bluffs, beaches, along rivers which flow into the sea and on islands which rise up from it. They are a great part of the delight of our planet and come in all varieties: the surprises of scale and shape and location make travel a wonder and a pleasure. This variety, however, has become endangered. When our lawmakers write laws or our planners make plans, they too often seek to discover the things that are the same about places and to legislate more sameness still. I know planners who believe that a single set of standards might apply, for instance, to the whole California coast. We must protect the shore—but not by destroying the variety that makes the waterfront such a special place. What we need is a positive force which introduces and interlaces the widest variety of public and private uses and densities and forms, rather than negative restrictions which limit those uses. I can see one universally desirable regulation: a regulation recognizing the value of the shore and forbidding its use for activities that do not benefit from a location by the sea.

In the coastal cities that I have described, human additions have enhanced this special location. The repeated message of this collection of wonders is that variety, a choreography of different excitements, creates waterfronts that are special places —each one memorable and different from all the others. ●

Lower Slaughter, in the Cotswolds in the west of England, is a tiny and very pretty village built along an open space through which a little river runs. The stream does what the road could never do: beckoning us to follow it down to the ocean.

CAROL A. FOOTE

In Venice, Italy (above), water within the city has been a tradition for hundreds of years. More recent developments have sought to capture the magic of the integration of water and urban development. An especially successful modern example is the Paseo Del Rio—the Downtown River Walk—in San Antonio, Texas, pictured at right above. Along the banks of the meandering San Antonio River, the visitor can find shopping, restaurants, and nightclubs amid banana trees and passing "river taxis." The fanciest of all such developments, Venice, California (seen at right in 1908) was an enormous fantasy that ultimately failed.

The Urban Edge

"The lazy blue sea sending its subdued rumble to the ear: the islands floating like a mirage upon its bosom, evokes the noble panorama of Camaldoli, or Positano, of Nervi, of Bordighera."

Ernest Peixotto[1]

A View From the Past:
The Shifting Images of Coastal California

DAVID GEBHARD

California, and especially the coast of California, has always had as much to do with romance and myth as it has had with fact. In truth it is close to impossible for visitors or residents to experience the relationship between ocean and coast except through a layered series of ideological glasses. But these layers of romance have not always been the same, nor, for that matter, have they always been present. The history of European settlement of California, from the eighteenth century to the present, has similarities with other coastal transformations throughout the world, but at the same time has been unique.

The Pacific coast of California is composed of a series of narrow, fragile environments, which, as with many of the lands adjoining the Mediterranean Sea, do not in most instances extend for any great distance into the continent. But the coastal regions of California reveal a number of worlds which are in stark contrast to the Mediterranean lands. The coast north of San Francisco Bay to the Oregon border, with its distinct climate—cold ocean currents, incessant strong winds, swirling heavy fogs—and its equally distinct land environment—high cliffs, low mountains pressing to the sea, and extensive coniferous forests—is not what most people imagine when they conjure up a vision of the California coast. The low rocky coast of Monterey and Carmel, with windblown cypress trees, and the warm sandy beaches of Malibu and Santa Monica are the usual images that come to mind when one thinks of coastal California.

Though the California coast is indeed composed of a remarkable array of micro-elements, each with its own distinct personality, the effect of Europeans, since the entrance of Spain to the south and Russia to the north, has been that of trying to erase these distinctions. The siting of cities, of groups of structures or single buildings, and of architectural images, has generally sought to destroy this variety, and through uniformity not only to tie the whole coast together, but to suggest the unity of California with the rest of America and of Europe.

The Unfriendly Shore

The Spanish, and later on the Mexicans, viewed the Pacific Ocean as a transportation corridor—an umbilical cord which attached this sparsely settled region to the "civilized" lands of Mexico and Spain. The eighteenth and early nineteenth century Hispanic coastal settlements, whether Mission churches or presidios, were always built some distance from the ocean. The coast itself was not a place to live near. The weather was considered far too cold, damp, and windy, and while the ocean was the benevolent connective link with civilization, it could also serve those who were unfriendly—marauding pirates or the ships and men of hostile nations. The coastal enclaves that the Hispanic peoples created in California were essentially inland-oriented communities. The ocean presence was manifest by the effect of the Pacific currents on the land, but it was not an element that usually made its visual presence felt. There were, to be sure, a few exceptions. The Presidio and Mission Church of Santa Barbara were situated in the upper reaches of a coastal valley so that they could enjoy a view of the ocean and the Channel Islands beyond. Yet the other Mission complexes in Santa Barbara County—la Purisma Concepcion Mission near Lompoc and the Santa Inez Mission—like most missions, were established in inland

From the 1870s on, people viewed the shore as a place for recreation and enjoyment, especially "bathing." Many recreational piers, bathhouses, and other facilities catering to tourists, vacationers, and the public at large were built from the late nineteenth century well into the twentieth. In the 1930 aerial photograph at right above, the popular Santa Monica Pier, Ocean Park Pier, and Venice Pier jut out into the bay from the Santa Monica / Venice shoreline. The photograph below shows the crowds attracted by such waterfront amenities.

E-4290-22

Photographed JULY 13, 1930 App 2:15 P.M
TIDE AT 2:15 P.M.

valleys. The land from the beach or cliff inland a mile or so was basically unoccupied during the late eighteenth and early nineteenth centuries.

As to the buildings themselves, the Hispanic settlers, in a fashion classic for colonists throughout history, sought to recreate as closely as possible the buildings with which they were familiar in Mexico or in distant Spain. For a rough frontier area, it is surprising how up-to-date some of the churches were. In structure, lack of sumptuous ornamentation and craftsmanship, they were admittedly provincial. But the images used—the late Churrigueresque of Mexico and the then-fashionable Neo-Classic—were not that different from what was being used in Spain and Mexico. The Santa Barbara Mission Church or the Chapel of San Francisco de Asis, with classical columned and pedimented facades, would not have been seen as "out of date" in any one of the smaller towns in Andalusian Spain or Mexico.

Whether built north of San Francisco Bay, as with San Francisco Solano in Sonoma, or San Diego de Alcala in San Diego, the Mission Churches and their surrounding buildings were meant to convey uniformity. San Carlos Borromeo might be situated in the lower reaches of the Monterey Peninsula, and San Luis Rey de Francia placed among the gentle rolling hills of southern California, two very different coastal environments, yet the design of the buildings was meant to deny these differences.

The sense of the ocean and the immediate coast as an unfriendly place continued unabated through the mid-nineteenth century. To be sure, the newly arrived Anglos brought a new set of architectural images which they employed in a fashion identical to the Hispanic peoples who had preceded them. Greek Revival, either as shimmery white clapboard buildings or as adobe structures modified by Classical elements, began to dot the coast. But the northern Cali-fornia coastal village of Mendocino, with its white clapboard houses and Masonic Hall (1865) and its siting on a high bluff, does not offer anything approaching the intimate contact between sea and land which one experiences in a New England seaside village.[2]

South of Mendocino, the coastal landscape was dotted with green shuttered, white clapboard Greek Revival houses, churches, and other buildings. Most of these structures looked not to the ocean but towards the land itself. Even those located close to the coast, like the small Trussell-Winchester house in Santa Barbara (1854) or the much grander Banning House in San Pedro (1864), were not sited or designed to establish a clear visual rapport with the nearby ocean.

The Coast and the Roller Coaster

Changes in how the coast might be used began to come to the fore in the 1870s, due to an inland phenomenon—the completion of the transcontinental railroads and the continuation of spur lines leading to or along the coast. The perception of the ocean as something to view, and especially in the southland as a place to bathe, was a major shift in public awareness. Coastal California was no longer a distinct frontier—it could now become a resort area, like the Riviera of France, the Brighton coast of England, or the New Jersey shoreland.

At first this new approach to the coast was gingerly. The Arlington Hotel in Santa Barbara (designed in 1865 by Peter J. Barber), the first coastal resort hotel, was sited halfway between the Mission Church and the harbor. In the north, the Hotel del Monte (designed by Arthur Brown, Sr. and built by the Pacific Improvement Company in 1879) was situated in the woods of the Monterey Peninsula, away from the sea. Though the del Monte was described as a ". . . monster hotel

The elaborate Moorish bathhouse built around the turn of the century on the Santa Monica beach is the epitome of the grand bathhouse style typical of the period.

HISTORICAL.

of quaint Swiss architecture,"[3] it, like the Arlington in Santa Barbara, was simply a reasonably fashionable variation of the then-popular Eastlake Style (the Stick Style). Similarly-designed hotels were being built in the Northeast and throughout the United States, so there was nothing distinct in either plan or detail about these early California coastal hotels.

Though the beauty of the natural environment of the Monterey Peninsula and of the south-facing Santa Barbara coast were themselves major inducements, it was not accidental that both of those locales also possessed "quaint" relics of non-Anglo history—the Hispanic village of Monterey, and the Mission Church and adobes of Santa Barbara. George A. Crofutt in his 1880 *New Overland Tourist and Pacific Coast Guide* described Monterey as ". . . a quiet, sleepy old town . . . living on in the dreamy self-satisfied consciousness that the spirit of progress is at an end. . . ."[4] And Mary Cone noted in her 1876 *Two Years in California,* "To the traveler from the east who makes Santa Barbara the first stopping place in southern California, it has a very foreign look . . . with its old adobe houses that look as though they had a heavy burden to support in the clumsy tiles which perform the office of roof for them."[5]

The lure of the coast in the 1870s, 1880s, and 1890s, whether in southern Europe or in California, was decidedly not a universal middle class dream. Rather it was as Crofutt observed ". . . for the better class of citizens . . . ," that is, the upper middle class and the wealthy.[6] Whether one lived in San Francisco and took the train down to Monterey, or came by trans-continental rail, the urge to go to the coast was prompted by the desire to regain one's health, to escape the day-to-day pressures of business or simply to clip one's coupons and have a pleasurable time.

By the 1890s, the coast of California south of San Francisco Bay was dotted with resort hotels. Santa Cruz came to be referred to as the "Newport of California" because of its hotels, and by 1890 it boasted the large Sea Beach Hotel.[7] The boom of the 1880s in southern California sprinkled the coast from Santa Monica Bay to Coronado with beach-oriented resort hotels.[8] As with other hotels constructed throughout the Southland, these coastal hostelries were built not simply as resorts on the beach, but as the principal incumbent within often extensive land development schemes. The prime *raison d'etre* of the hotels was as a symbolic drawing card, to encourage the purchase of the adjoining land for residential and commercial purposes.

As with the hotels of the earlier decade, those of the end of the 1880s employed an imported Anglo style, the Queen Anne Revival. They created a romantic silhouette posed against the waters of the Pacific—a picturesque silhouette composed of varied roofs, gables, and dormers, broken by turrets and towers. The Del Coronado in Coronado made a slight gesture to regionalism through its interior courtyard, but on the whole these shingle and clapboard "piles" perfectly matched those in the East, the South, and the Midwest.

Another ingredient taken from the East was the association of the sea with the late nineteenth century phenomenon of the amusement park. As in the East, the coastal amusement park marked the first major inroad of the middle and "artisan" classes into the beach area. Santa Cruz abandoned any pretense to be the West's Newport and built its first roller coaster in 1884. By the early 1880s Santa Monica and nearby Venice had their pleasure piers and other amusements. A closely related episode which compromised the elitism of the beach was the introduction of bathhouses and entire tent cities on the beaches. At first these were private, such as the Sutro Baths in San Francisco; but public bath houses were later built in Santa Barbara and elsewhere. More and more, the beach was becoming a playground for all people.

The Hotel del Coronado, near San Diego on the southern coast, like many of the period, was a grand design based on the popular but imported Queen Anne Revival style. Such a hotel would be as much at home in the prairies of the midwest as on the shore of the ocean.

LIZA RIDDLE

The Coast and the Middle Class

In general, the mid- to late-nineteenth century Anglo cities laid out on the coast were pure and simple grid schemes. Along the northern coast, Eureka's 1850 grid plan made a slight nod to the non-cardinal points orientation of Humboldt Bay. In the south, Santa Monica's grid of 1875 could just as well have been in Kansas or Ohio, except for the boulevard directly atop the coastal cliff. But when a scheme was directed toward the upper middle class, the right angle geometry of the grid was modified or completely disregarded. The Coronado plan of 1886 exhibited grand boulevards, a central plaza, and a beach-oriented roadway, upon which were to be constructed "substantial" homes. Del Monte, with its famed 17 Mile Drive, mirrored the approach taken to irregular eighteenth century English picturesque gardens. The 17 Mile Drive itself was essentially a romantic wood-enshrouded road used for excursions from the hotel; by the turn of the century, retreats for the wealthy were being built along it and in other parts of the peninsula.

By the end of the 1880s, the woodsy vocabulary of the late Queen Anne and early Colonial Revival was being challenged by two very different approaches to design—the Craftsman bungalow and the Mission Revival with its reference to California's own regional past. The bungalow with its avowed "democratic" overtones suggested not only a return to the frontier life, but also the symbolism of the American ideal of a universal middle class. The bungalow represented one of California's twentieth century gifts to the world. That timber-poor Los Angeles, rather than San Francisco, became the recognized bungalow capital of America illustrates how modern production and transportation could easily destroy regional variations. The universalism of the bungalow built on the coast itself can be seen in Manhattan Beach, laid out in 1897, which was characterized as "a quiet bungalow colony." In nearby Long Beach, the brothers Charles and Henry Greene set one of their large two-story bungalows (for the Tichenor family, 1904) on top of the low cliff overlooking the ocean. Far to the north, in the coastal lumber town of Fort Bragg, a small colony of middle class bungalows was built (ca. 1910); and except for the northern vegetation, one could easily imagine being in Pasadena or Altadena.

The New World's Mediterranean Shore

The Mission Revival was California's first fling at regional independence from the fashions of the northeast. As with the bungalow, the center of it all was the Southland, reaching from San Diego to Santa Barbara. But the image of the Mission, with its plain white stucco walls, arched openings and red tile roofs, was not limited to the south. Mission Revival hotels, railroad stations, stores, bungalow courts, and dwellings were built throughout California, including the coastal zone. In the hands of a gifted designer such as Irving J. Gill, Mission villas were posed on the coastal cliffs of La Jolla not only as abstract geometric forms, but also as images which evoked the African and European coasts of the Mediterranean.

To a marked degree, the turn of the century Mission Revival represents California's first major effort to openly respond to the presence of the coast. The transformation of California into a new and improved Mediterranean world was bound up with horticulture, architectural images, and the "reality" of illusions. Initially, the Mission Revival referred to California's late eighteenth, early nineteenth century Hispanic past, but this was almost immediately broadened to include the Mediterranean coast of Italy, France, Spain, and North Africa. Southern California's Venice, with its canals, arched bridges, and its own version of the Doge's Palace, was laid out and partially built in 1904.[9] A little farther south, near Long Beach, the theme of Italy and canals appeared in Naples (founded in 1905).

It is difficult for us today to sense the general unanimity and intensity of the desire in the 1910s and 1920s to see California as the New World's Mediterranean shore. The hills and cliffs facing onto the Pacific were to be dotted with gleaming white-walled and red tile villas and hotels, and here and there were to be Spanish villages. San Clemente, on the coast near the ruins of California's largest Mission complex, the Mission San Juan Capistrano was conceived of in 1925 as "a village done in the Fashion of Old Spain."[10] The upper middle class suburban development of Palos Verdes (designed between 1922–1925 by Olmsted and Olmsted) was to be planned around several Spanish villages (only one of which was built, Malaga Cove Plaza).[11] The most perfect allusion to the coast of Mediterranean Spain and France, with their mountains

dropping down to the sea, occurred in Montecito, Santa Barbara, and Hope Ranch. Here, Bertram G. Goodhue, George Washington Smith, and other architects sited their hillside villas so that from the ocean they did indeed look like a watercolor landscape sketched in southern France by Paul Cezanne.

The Mediterranean illusion was carried north to the Monterey Peninsula. In 1925, the Monterey Peninsula Country Club at Pebble Beach was laid out, and during the remaining years of the decade, Mediterranean villas were built on the hills overlooking the golf course and directly on the cliffs above the water. These included a wide array of Mediterranean modes, ranging from the highly personal interpretations of Bernard Maybeck (Ford House, Pebble Beach, 1922) to California's only Byzantine villa, the Fagan / Crocker House (1924–28) designed by George Washington Smith.

The unanimity of the Mediterranean, whether Spanish or Italian, was never, of course, total. Other historic allusions to America's and California's European heritage occurred during the 1920s and 1930s. In Oceanside, north of San Diego, the St. Malo Club (1929) established a 27-acre beachfront enclave whose architecture was French Norman, with the houses having picturesque steep roofs and walls of rough brick, cobblestone, half timber and stucco. Carmel Village, which emerged after 1900 as California's Bohemian hideaway, leaned towards the Hansel and Gretel world of the medieval fairy tale and doll house.

The Twentieth Century Coast

Both in land planning and in the realm of architectural imagery, the decade of the 1930s perfectly represented "laissez-faire-ism." Stretches of the coast emerged as closely-packed beach colonies displaying the full gamut of architectural imagery, ranging from continuations of historic illusionisms to the new allusions to the Machine—both Streamline Moderne (Art Deco) and Modern. At Sea Cliff, south of Santa Cruz, a group of Streamline Modern houses posed as ocean liners stranded on the beach. In the south, narrow strands of beachlands at Carpinteria, Malibu, and Santa Monica housed an amazing potpourri of architectural images. White painted board and batten green cottages were situated next to clapboard shuttered Colonial Revival houses, which in turn might be adjacent to the curved forms of a stucco, steel, and glass Modern Moderne house. Though their images were on the catholic side, these divergent forms were reasonably unified in scale and in their orientation towards the beach and the ocean surf.

The post World War II years, from the late 1940s through 1960, witnessed much of the same, except historic illusions declined and Modernism increased. With only a few exceptions, this version of Modernism conveyed a sense of easy-going livability, rather than the new twenty-first century Arcadia of the Machine. This shift reflects a different view of the coast and the ocean from that of the 1910s and 1920s. The romance of the Pacific Coast as the New Mediterranean, with its references to history and culture, was replaced by the narcissism of pleasure. The beach and the water were a place to play. Along stretches of the California coast, the state began to organize urban beaches and state parks; while in the private sector, marinas were built to provide waterside living and increased accommodations for pleasure craft. Both of these phenomena meant that more extensive sections of the actual beach would be open to the public—meaning the middle class and their children. The first marinas, in San Francisco Bay, in Ventura, and south to San Diego, were priced and directed to the middle class. All of these early marinas maintained the same low village scale that had occured in the earlier beach colonies. Like Cliff May's popular ranch house, the design of these usually attached dwellings was both lightly historic and modern, to symbolize the easygoing pleasure-oriented life of their inhabitants.

Though a few high-rise apartments had been built on the coast in communities such as Santa Monica in the 1930s, most of California's shoreline had remained relatively free of this twentieth century malady. Slowly in the 1960s and 1970s, the horizontal scale of California's coast began to be compromised by high-rise towers. In a few rare instances, such as in Louis I. Kahn's Salk Institute at La Jolla (1959–65), the towers composed themselves as an impressive modern castle, set alone high on a hill. But generally most of the slab high-rises built on the coast in the 1960s and 1970s have been bland to the extreme, and not only have they ruthlessly

destroyed the scale of the buildings around them, they have equally compromised the natural character of the coast itself. Approaching Santa Monica along the coast highway and seeing her increasing wall of high-rise towers serves only to remind us of other destroyed coastlines, whether on the east coast of Florida or along the Mediterranean coast of Spain. A few of California's coastal communities have sensed the devastating effect of high-rise buildings, and they have sought to prohibit them. La Jolla fought valiantly, but lost; Santa Barbara politely said no, and has stood firm.

The traditional view that the seaside should provide a retreat for the upper middle class continued on into the post World War II decades. The Sea Ranch development, located on the northern California coast, has received the acclaim of planners and architects. Though the ocean, cliffs, and wooded hills behind are spectacular, the climate is not. Cold winds and fog have always made this site, and the northern coast in general, an undesirable place to live. The triumph of the Sea Ranch is that in its initial planning (by Lawrence Halprin and Associates), and in the siting and design of the buildings (Joseph Esherick and Associates; Moore, Lyndon, Turnbull, Whitaker; and others), it solved many of the negative environmental problems.

The imagery employed at the Sea Ranch—that of the Woodsey Third Bay Tradition—played a fascinating visual game between traditionalism and the modern. Moore, Lyndon, Turnbull, Whitaker's Condominium I (1965), with its vertical "mineshaft" volumes topped by a multiplicity of shed roofs, quickly established a style which became the rage throughout the United States and abroad. Variations on the theme occurred all along the California coast from San Diego to San Francisco Bay and beyond. By the 70s, many of these Moore-esque designs (named for the architect Charles W. Moore) began to embrace the (Hispanic) Mediterranean imagery of California. In their site planning, and in their use of stucco walls and tile, there was more than a casual hint that once again we had a Spanish village by the sea. Moore himself openly suggested this connection in his Faculty Club at the University of California at Santa Barbara (1967); and the Bay Area firm of Fisher Friedman has indicated a similar direction in many of its condominium projects, of which Promontory Point (1973–74) at Newport Beach is a characteristic example.

In the late 1970s and now into the 1980s, California has, more intensely than the rest of the country, experienced a revival of Revivals. Historicism, of a sort, is now back in fashion. Only this time, the historian looks not to original sources, like California's own Hispanic adobes and Missions or the historic architecture of the Mediterranean. Rather, the backward look is now diverted to the Revival architecture of the 1920s. This is in a way outright nostalgia, in which architecture merely provides the needed stage sets. As elsewhere in the state, the coast now has its own recent array of Spanish, French Norman, and English half Tudor motels, restaurants, shopping centers, condominiums, and large family houses. Few of these are really carried out well—conviction and knowledge appear to be lacking in both client and architect. Certainly they do not express any new coherent sympathy with the coast of California as a special place. And this is true not only of the buildings themselves but is even more the case with their landscape architecture and planning concepts.

The Need for a Guiding Image

One need not be filled with nostalgia to sense that only during the years 1900 through the early 1930s was there a generally accepted positive view of how to respond to the coast. These years came close to success because the California coast was seen not directly but through the eyes of historical reference (and thereby historical continuity). The idea of what the coast symbolized was more significant than the actual fact of hills, beach, surf, and ocean. It was this theme which Moore embraced in Condominium I at the Sea Ranch. Similar themes have been hinted at in various coastal projects since then, but none of them has realized the potential suggested in the initial planning of the Sea Ranch. ●

Notes:

1. Ernest Peixotto, *Romantic California* (New York: Scribner's, 1917) p. 3.

2. Federal Writers' Project, U.P.A., *California: A Guide to the Golden State* (New York: Hastings House, 1954) p. 320.

3. Federal Writers' Project, U.P.A., *Monterey Peninsula* (Stanford: Stanford University Press, 1941) p. 56.

4. George A. Crofutt, *New Overland Tourist and Pacific Coast Guide* (Omaha: The Overland Publishing Co., 1880) p. 224.

5. Mary Cone, *Two Years in California* (Chicago: S. C. Griggs, 1876) pp. 89–90.

6. George A. Crofutt, *op. cit.*; p. 224.

7. John Chase, *The Sidewalk Companion to Santa Cruz Architecture* (Santa Cruz: Paper Vision Press, 1979, pp. 23–26.

8. Prominent among these were the Arcadia in Santa Monica (Boring and Haas, 1887), the Redondo in Redondo Beach (1887), the Long Beach in Long Beach (1884), and the still standing Del Coronado Hotel in Coronado (James W. and Merritt Reid, 1886–88).

9. Annette Del Zoppo and Jeffrey Stanton, *Venice California 1904–1930* (Venice: ARS Publications, 1978).

10. Homer Banks, *The Story of San Clemente* (Los Angeles: privately printed, 1930).

11. Charles H. Cheney, "Palos Verdes, Eight Years of Development," *The Architect and Engineer,* vol. 100 (January, 1938) pp. 35–83.

The Promontory Point development in Newport Beach (below) crowds residences together in an effort to maximize views of the surroundings. The inset above shows a splendid example of the Craftsman bungalow, this one in La Jolla and one of two which have been accorded historic site status. The Sea Ranch development, seen at left, is a spectacularly successful design achieved by taking into account the siting and climate to solve a variety of environmental problems.

Section Two
Making Changes on the Waterfront

Almost without exception, the examples of sound coastal design cited in Section One describe development which appears to fit its setting. This does not always mean that design must be hidden from view. In his essay, Charles Moore points out that design for human activity can enhance a site, adding to the natural setting. But enhancement is a quality that is subject to opinion and thus difficult to treat by regulation. What one person considers an enhancement, another may consider obtrusive.

For this reason, the aim of California's coastal program has been to subordinate new construction in rural areas to its surroundings; and to require new construction on urban waterfronts to be compatible with the type and scale of existing structures and uses. The Coastal Act also requires that development encourage public use and enjoyment of the coast, and wherever possible, requires new development to preserve and encourage traditional coastal activities—fishing, shipping, water-oriented recreation, and other activities that are dependent on a coastal location. The Coastal Act's designation of these activities as priority uses preserves not only the aesthetic diversity of the waterfront but its economic diversity as well.

In Section Two, we examine several mechanisms which have successfully effected positive changes in California's urban waterfronts: regulation, positive government action, and citizen participation. In the first article, William M. Boyd describes the principles for coastal design developed by the California Coastal Commission since its inception in 1973. He examines influences on the decisions of the Commission and the results of these decisions in specific instances.

Sally Woodbridge examines the Coastal Commission's regulatory actions from the designer's perspective. In two case studies, she describes the Commission's policies and guidelines, which created a framework of limitations within which the architect could design a structure or a project. The regulatory process adds to the designer's responsibilities: the designer is obligated to be aware of Coastal Act requirements and must communicate them to the client. By taking the Commission's concerns into account and designing a structure that harmonizes with its environment, a designer will minimize permit denials and will, in the long run, save the client time and money.

Regulation provides limitations to design, but not inspiration. Gray Brechin describes projects in which the public sector has acted to inspire and encourage good design projects. Brechin describes a project involving several San Francisco departments together with the San Francisco Bay Conservation and Development Commission (BCDC), and another by the State Coastal Conservancy. Each can serve as a model for future projects by public agencies.

Joseph E. Petrillo and Peter Grenell take us through several additional projects of the State Coastal Conservancy. These projects demonstrate how "positive" government action may be required to resolve coastal conflicts, and demonstrate a concerted effort to encourage excellence of design in urban waterfront areas.

The coastal community itself has served as a source of design inspiration. Peter Brand discusses the theory and practice of community participation in coastal design projects. Brand describes in detail a community participation project in Seal Beach, where citizens completed a redevelopment plan for an unused coastal site. Local controversy over the site was resolved by proposing a project that met community needs for public amenities, and was still economically self-supporting. The citizens' plan also joined aesthetic and economic benefits with compatible design, public access to the shoreline, and coastal recreation—a happy union all too rarely achieved by "professional" designers and developers.

Finally, Jim Burns encourages readers to think about how their own communities could be improved and describes how people can begin to analyze community needs. Taking a close look at several communities on the California coast, Burns examines the advantages, problems, and potentials of each town and points out ways that each could be improved.

Together, these essays discuss successful approaches to resolution of land use conflicts and design problems in an area of environmental sensitivity–the California coast.

Coastal Regulation:
Assuring Access to California's Coast

WILLIAM M. BOYD

Under the 1972 and 1976 coastal acts, design review at the state level differs markedly from the design review function generally performed by planning commissions, city councils, and boards of supervisors at the local government level. Local government hearings on development permits often focus on typical design issues, such as architectural style and exterior materials. In contrast, design review by the State Coastal Commission has tended to focus on site planning, particularly on preserving visual access to the coast and on assuring meaningful access to the waterfront. Even when considering the more traditional design issues, such as the overall scale of development, the State Coastal Commission has tended to focus on a specific definable concern, such as the danger that a large new development will overpower a historic structure in the same area.

The Credibility of Design Review–The Vagaries of Aesthetics in the Regulatory System

It is fair to say that the subjectivity of aesthetic regulation makes it inherently suspect in the development industry, particularly where developers perceive that it is being used as a device to reduce project densities as a form of down-zoning. This has often been the case on the California coast. Therefore the development of defined, coastal-oriented design principles has been important in establishing the credibility of the Commission's design review. Presently, no clear legal standards govern the exercise of "police power" discretion in matters of aesthetics.[1]

In this chapter, we examine the evolution of the Commission's design review principles and describe some past and present applications of these principles.

The Evolution of Coastal Design Review Policies

The diversity of California's coastline reflects the legendary, some would say notorious, diversity of the Golden State's lifestyles. A secluded cove on the Big Sur shoreline is a world removed from the broad expanses of Santa Monica's crowded beaches. However, one fact unifies the perceptions of the California coast: over 85 percent of the state's population lives within 30 miles of the coast. The coast is a central feature in the lifestyle that has drawn the massive in-migration to California. Fundamental to this lifestyle is the need to see and use the coast.

It would seem that residents of a state with a 1,100-mile coastline would be able to see and use it. But both the size and concentration of California's major urban areas—San Diego, Los Angeles / Orange County, San Francisco Bay Area—have created tremendous pressures on the use of the coast. Moreover, the essentially laissez-faire system of land use which preceeded the passage of Proposition 20 often led to the sale and exclusive use of parts of the coast by the highest bidders. A classic example of the coast as a private enclave is the Malibu coast, immediately to the north of Los Angeles. Here, modest structures of enormous real estate value have been built cheek-by-jowl. We can drive along Pacific Coast Highway in Malibu in a classic Mediterranean setting, but we can't see our "Mediterranean."

The years immediately preceding the passage of Proposition 20 witnessed a headlong rush toward literally "walling off" the coast. In southern California, the natural attraction of the coast was reinforced by the marked superiority of coastal air quality over the brown haze that now frequently envelops formerly smog-free prestigious areas like Pasadena.

R. VALENTINE ATKINSON

The aerial view at right shows the heart of Monterey's downtown waterfront area, which contains a mix of new development and restoration of historic structures. At upper center is the new publicly developed Conference Center with pedestrian access through a cluster of restored historic buildings to the commercially successful Fisherman's Wharf. Located at the base of the wharf is the Custom House (left), built in 1827, which typifies the town's colonial architectural heritage.

Waterfront areas that were not prime residential areas ten years ago now have homes selling for $750,000. In the early 1970s, wall-to-wall locked gate communities were built in formerly small towns within commuting distance of major urban centers, such as Solana Beach in San Diego County. Closer-in urban areas created a market for massive high rise complexes, such as Coronado Shores near San Diego. A common feature even of publicly financed redevelopment plans in areas such as Santa Monica and Redondo Beach was high-density residential projects, with limited visual and physical access through the project areas.

In northern California, pressures were exerted more in the direction of large second-home subdivisions in rural areas rather than primary residences in urban areas. Amid much controversy, the Sea Ranch development received approval to build 5,000 units of housing and to close off ten miles of coastline to future public access. (In return, the developers dedicated a large park at the northern edge of the project area.) Not only was ten miles of coastline closed off to public use, a tree screen was planted seaward of the main coast road in such a way that magnificent views of the ocean were effectively walled off by a screen of vegetation.

Loss of visual and physical access was clearly a strong force behind the passage of Proposition 20 in November 1972. The passage of the coastal initiative by a majority in Los Angeles County, an area not generally inclined toward strict land use regulation, attests to the strong desire to protect the urban as well as the rural coast.

On the coast, the object of aesthetic protection is defined: the unique meeting of land and water. If a person says, "I want to see the ocean," the parameters of regulation are, in a sense, defined. In November of 1972, 55 percent of the California electorate said "we want to be able to see the ocean and to be able to reach it."

The extent to which a project preserves public views and provides physical access can be verified independently. Major views of the coast from public areas can be mapped. Potential public access areas can be outlined on site. The size and location of plazas and parks involve some degree of subjective judgment, but often even such major use areas are defined by their relationship to significant vistas of small craft harbors or natural scenic amenities and to other present or potential accessways. Policy criteria in the Coastal Act of 1976 may not be as precise as a zoning ordinance, but they are much more defined than the typical design review comment that the project "doesn't feel right."

Even so, in a state with widely differing aesthetic values and approaches to development, determining how coastal land use regulation should be applied to highly subjective development design issues was not a simple matter. Proposition 20 gave little specific guidance; the four objectives of the 1972 initiative were phrased in the broadest of terms. The generality of the Act's provisions can be seen in one of the few policy sections of the Act:

> 27302. The coastal zone plan shall be consistent with all of the following objectives:
> (a) The maintenance, restoration, and enhancement of the overall quality of the Coastal zone environment, including, but not limited to, its amenities and aesthetic values.

Nowhere in the Act were terms such as "amenities" and "aesthetic values" defined. However, the Act did provide that certain kinds of projects required a two-thirds vote of the Commission, as contrasted with the normal majority vote, thereby indicating that these kinds of development impacts required special attention. Among projects requiring a two-thirds vote were:

A wall of dreary, monotonous bungalows blocks ocean views and beach access from busy Pacific Coast Highway (Highway 1) along the Malibu coast. This type of uninspired development helped spur the passage of Proposition 20 in 1972.

LIZA RIDDLE

(d) Any development which would substantially interfere with or detract from the lein of sight toward the sea from the state highway nearest the coast.

The permit process established under the initiative defined the scope and content of virtually all policy issues raised under Proposition 20, including issues related to design regulation. Since all development located within 1,000 yards of the shoreline required a coastal permit, the staff of the Coastal Commission, charged with the job of issuing these permits, had to cope with an enormous array of design issues.

The Coastal Commission's approach to design review was influenced to a great degree by its composition. The widely varying backgrounds and geographic spectrum represented by the Commissioners created a forum for policy formulation that served as a true "melting pot" of ideas where no one viewpoint could dominate. The Commissioners' part-time rather than full-time status forced them to concentrate on only the most central policy issues; they could not afford to be distracted by the detailed design review that often occurred at the regional commissions. A practical, but very real, influence sharpening the focus of the Commission project review process was the limited hearing time available for each project—a 3,000-unit project might be reviewed in less than an hour simply because the Commission had to review projects from all over the state while continuing its work on State Coastal Plan formulation, in accordance with the stringent time limits established by Proposition 20.

The essence of coastal design review can be distilled from a number of Coastal Act permit decisions.

In rural areas, development must be subordinate to the natural setting and must not interfere with major public views to and along the coast. In areas such as Big Sur, a number of siting techniques have evolved to help facilitate compliance with these requirements, including the use of berms, sod roofs, natural materials, etc.[2]

In urban areas, development does not have to be subordinate to natural features, but must be compatible with the primary coastal attributes of the area such as: 1) historic structures, 2) scale of the community in relation to coastal scenic qualities, or 3) water-related uses such as fishing piers. Where there is no defined physical amenity, the Commission stresses maintaining or enhancing public views of the coast.

Learning through Experience–The First Results

Early attempts at defining the role of the Commission in reviewing project siting and project design were not overly successful. One of the first permit applications was for residential development on a bluff overlooking a state beach in southern Orange County. The Commission was sympathetic to the plight of a developer caught in midstream by the passage of Proposition 20, and no re-design was required. Instead, the developer was required to dedicate a blufftop view park. The view park does provide visual access to the coast. However, the completed project intrudes visually into the backdrop of the park and detracts substantially from the pleasures of being at the oceanfront.

In another project approved early in the Commission's history, consideration of scenic impacts and siting was subordinated to other policy objectives. A project proposed for a scenic agricultural valley to the south of Santa Barbara presented an opportunity to establish the policy tradeoff: the Commission allowed development to be clustered at a relatively high density on one portion of a parcel in return for the dedication of a larger portion for permanent open space preservation. Unfortunately, in the desire to establish this principle, the Commission's staff did not pay sufficient attention to the visual impact that the project would have on the valley as a whole. The staff did not properly consider the project in relation to its setting and the completed project represents a major visual intrusion into a rural setting. Commission staff learned the hard way from that project that projects in rural areas must be subordinate to their setting and cannot be allowed to intrude on the dominant physical characteristics of the area.

The coastal permit review process also provided essential experience in learning to determine the proper scope of design review in urban settings. One of the first major urban permit applications was the Monterey Redevelopment Agency's proposal to construct a major conference center in an area between downtown Monterey and the waterfront, in a designated Urban Renewal Area near the Monterey pier. The proposed project included not only a hotel and convention center but also a civic auditorium.[3] The auditorium's highest point would have been close to that of the highest building in Monterey. The site of the proposed project was immediately across the street from historic adobes dating from colonial days and adjacent to the low-rise historic Custom House and plaza that had been very successfully restored.

The Monterey Conference Center Project is discussed in detail in Chapter 4. Here we would like only to note a few relevant points about the final design. First, the issue of scale was dealt with by eliminating the visually intrusive civic auditorium, resulting in a profile in harmony with the adjoining Custom House. Second, the architectural design in general maintains the physicial integrity of the historic character that distinguishes Monterey from the "cuteness" of areas such as

Carmel, which lack the underlying character created by a true physical connection with the past. Finally, the Center illustrates another key concept in coastal design review policies: the creation of pedestrian linkages from urban centers to the shoreline. The final design incorporates a pedestrian access protected from automobile intrusion that had not previously existed.

Providing Access and Protecting Views

Two projects best exemplify what the Coastal Commission was attempting to achieve through site plan review in urban areas.

The Redondo Beach Redevelopment Project is located in one of the beach towns that formerly served as recreational retreats for old Los Angeles. Like other nearby beach towns, Redondo Beach is now part of the Los Angeles metropolitan complex and has witnessed intense condominium development in the oceanfront area. The first phases of the Redondo Beach redevelopment project enhanced public access to some degree by providing a major parking garage and a boardwalk along one portion of the waterfront. But the residential portion of the project blocked all but fleeting views of the ocean from Catalina Avenue, the main road paralleling the coast. The project did not provide substantial public use areas or any usable pedestrian access other than the boardwalk. The last phases of the project site plan would have been a series of high-rise apartments with no pedestrian access linking Catalina Avenue with the boardwalk area. The passage of Proposition 20 effectively halted this last phase, leading to litigation between the City of Redondo Beach and the Coastal Commission over the city's claim to "vested rights" to complete the project.

Faced with the prospect of a long legislative fight over the enactment of permanent coastal legislation in 1976, the Coastal Commission staff decided in 1975 to resolve the dispute over the remaining phases of the Redondo Beach Redevelopment Project. Initial site visits convinced the staff that meaningful physical and visual access could be provided while still allowing substantial development opportunities. The walkways and bikepath along Catalina Avenue could be linked with the previously constructed boardwalk along the harbor, which was in turn connected with the city pier and parking structure. A three-acre park with picnic and strolling areas with views of the small craft harbor could also be provided.

The site plan for the project as approved by the Coastal Commission shows how the site planning concepts of pedestrian linkages and preservation of view corridors were carried out. In contrast with a pedestrian walkway that winds almost

hidden through or near the residential area, the three-acre park is a broad, open expanse that invites public use. The Commission's primary concerns in the siting of the adjoining residential development were: 1) to avoid any de facto intimidation of public use by setting development back from the park, and 2) to preserve the three mapped view corridors, two of which extend right through the residential areas. While the Commission did require some re-design of residential exteriors, the only involvement in details was the specification that the project have all-wood exteriors. Their theory was that even if the final architectural plans were less than impressive, the all-wood exteriors would weather and could be landscaped to minimize visual conflict with the park. Interestingly enough, the developer (Lincoln Properties) responded to Commission requirements with architectural designs far superior to any of the other developments located in the area and to the first phases of its own project. Thus the State Coastal Commission's design review process focused on: 1) providing continuous public access to and along the coast, primarily through linked pedestrian accessways, and 2) assuring public views of the oceanfront.

The Redondo Beach Redevelopment Project shows how a project site plan was totally re-designed to provide access and

Cleverly disguised oil derricks (top) in Long Beach harbor attempt to provide a striking sculptural alternative to unadorned industrial structures.

Top: One of three view corridors required by the Coastal Commission in the Redondo Beach Redevelopment Project assures public views of the waterfront. Bottom: An earlier development in the same area, without such a requirement, illustrates the complete loss of such oceanfront views.

preserve views. In many other cases, site plan review does not require major re-design but only modifications. In 1978, the City of Long Beach presented to the Coastal Commission plans for an 18-story convention hotel. The conditions approved by the Commission included a requirement that a boardwalk planned as part of the project be extended at its inland terminus to connect with downtown Long Beach and at its other end to link with the shoreline rather than terminate at an overpass. In its findings, the Coastal Commission noted:

> The conditions *do not affect the basic design or location of the hotel* and its required facilities but require the City to provide *a more balanced development;* providing *more public coastally oriented activities and access* [emphasis added]. . . . The conditions required by this permit assure that coastal access is maximized by the construction of the entire Boardwalk from Ocean Boulevard to the shoreline simultaneously with the hotel development.

The Long Beach convention hotel also illustrates how design review under the Coastal Act is much more concerned with preserving and enhancing public views than it is with specific architectural design. The Commission found:

> The location of an 18-story hotel tower and the additional facilities on the immediate shoreline is a difficult design task. The site plan maximizes the view potential for the rooms in the tower and places the subsidiary hotel structures in front of the public open area and shops. The appellants are concerned that the tower unnecessarily intrudes into the Lagoon and will block public views from the existing Convention Center. The City has made a convincing case that the location of the tower in this site is critical to the economic viability of the entire project. To accommodate the City's concerns and still provide viewing areas for the general public, this permit requires that the public area where the Boardwalk extends south of the shopping mall and hotel be expanded to provide public views from additional eating areas and a plaza. This is the area which will provide the best coastal views and must be oriented to the ocean. The conditions and the revised site plan will more clearly separate hotel related uses from the more publicly oriented activities than the proposed plan.

As shown in these two examples, design review in urban areas has focused on assuring that significant public views of the coast are maintained. In Long Beach, this objective was achieved by improving the siting of public viewing areas. In

The Urban Edge

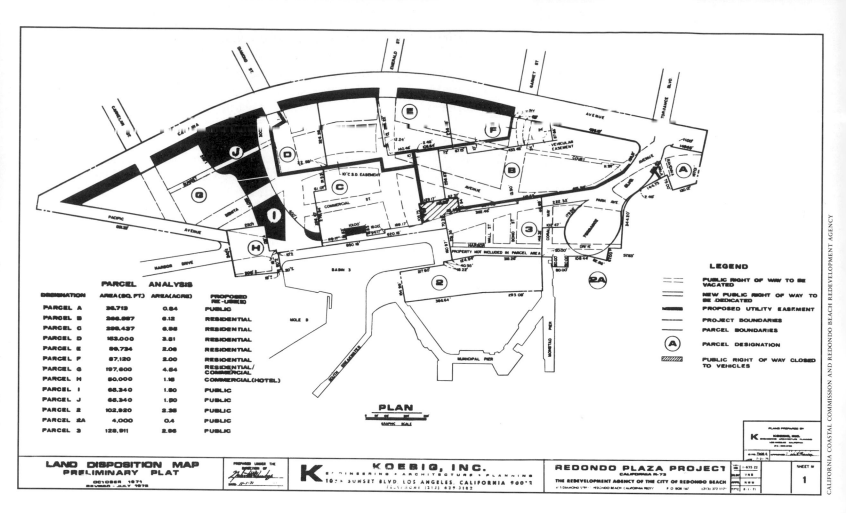

PARCEL ANALYSIS

DESIGNATION	AREA (SQ. FT.)	AREA (ACRE)	PROPOSED RE-USE(S)
PARCEL A	36,713	0.84	PUBLIC
PARCEL B	266,667	6.12	RESIDENTIAL
PARCEL C	298,437	6.85	RESIDENTIAL
PARCEL D	153,000	3.51	RESIDENTIAL
PARCEL E	89,734	2.06	RESIDENTIAL
PARCEL F	87,120	2.00	RESIDENTIAL
PARCEL G	197,600	4.54	RESIDENTIAL/COMMERCIAL
PARCEL H	50,000	1.15	COMMERCIAL (HOTEL)
PARCEL I	65,340	1.50	PUBLIC
PARCEL J	65,340	1.50	PUBLIC
PARCEL 2	102,920	2.36	PUBLIC
PARCEL 2A	4,000	0.4	PUBLIC
PARCEL 3	128,911	2.96	PUBLIC

PLAN

GRAPHIC SCALE

LEGEND

— — — PUBLIC RIGHT OF WAY TO BE VACATED

—— NEW PUBLIC RIGHT OF WAY TO BE DEDICATED

▬▬ PROPOSED UTILITY EASEMENT

—— PROJECT BOUNDARIES

—— PARCEL BOUNDARIES

(A) PARCEL DESIGNATION

▨ PUBLIC RIGHT OF WAY CLOSED TO VEHICLES

LAND DISPOSITION MAP
PRELIMINARY PLAT
OCTOBER 1971
REVISED — JULY 1972

KOEBIG, INC.
ENGINEERING • ARCHITECTURE • PLANNING
SUNSET BLVD. LOS ANGELES, CALIFORNIA 90012

REDONDO PLAZA PROJECT
CALIFORNIA R-72
THE REDEVELOPMENT AGENCY OF THE CITY OF REDONDO BEACH

SHEET
1

The aerial view at left shows the first phase of development of the Redondo Plaza project in the city of Redondo Beach. At top is the revised land disposition map and site plan for this project showing the provision for continuous physical access to the waterfront required by the Coastal Commission. The Coastal Commission also required a three-acre blufftop park (inset) with picnic and strolling areas and ocean views. This park is part of the continuous physical access requirement illustrated in the site plan above.

Redondo Beach, private development was reoriented so that it did not intrude on defined view corridors. In both cases, designs were modified by adding public use areas and/or by setting buildings back from public spaces to avoid any sense that the public is intruding on private uses. A close look at the Redondo Beach project reveals that the public view corridors through the project site also allowed the developer to maximize the number of residential units with harbor and ocean views, bringing a commensurate view premium to the developer.

Conclusion–Design Review as Site Planning

For those unfamiliar with the tremendous pressures exerted by economic forces toward "privatizing" the coast, it may seem that the preceding discussion regarding the central role of the principles of view protection and public access in coastal design review is overstated. It may seem obvious that the public should be able to see and have access to the oceanfront and that accordingly, coastal design review would simply be able to assume that visual and physical access would be provided in all major projects. Under such assumptions, it would be possible to focus coastal design regulation on other matters such as architectural design principles. However, such assumptions are not realistic in the context of the enormous market pressures and the demand for "coastal views" and developments "right on the waterfront."

If the past ten years of design review in California under the nation's strongest coastal land use regulatory system are indicative of future concerns, it is likely that coastal design review will continue to focus on view protection and physical access as the central issues, rather than other areas of design review. The following experience of the Coastal Commission in reviewing a hotel project in southern Orange County illustrates how site planning for public use areas continues to be the focus of the Commission's attention.

In 1979, the Coastal Commission approved in concept a 3,000-unit residential development on the Orange County coast that also included a major hotel facility on a coastal bluff, a blufftop park, and access trails. The hotel, park, and trails were considered major improvements in a project which had been previously denied twice. One reason for earlier denials was the proposed use for private residences of all the blufftop areas, overlooking a public beach. The Coastal Act places a high priority on visitor-serving uses in oceanfront areas, and the addition of hotel, park, and trails fit with this priority.

However, between the concept and the final plans, a few significant changes were introduced, either by design or by accident. The final plans for the hotel portion of the project had relocated the blufftop view park from a place where it would have been visible from the beach to a location behind one of the wings of the hotel. The final plans also eliminated a proposed accessway from a parking lot to the park. These design changes would have effectively converted a public plaza into a private park for hotel guests. At the same time, the revised plans had severely restricted potential views from the blufftop park by inserting a building between the park and the upcoast views. When these revisions came to the attention of the Commission staff, the developer was required to revise the final plans to conform with the original design, thereby retaining the visibility of the park from the beach to enhance its accessibility and to provide the best possible upcoast and downcoast views.

In the Commission's view, the relative importance of view protection/public access clearly outweighs the importance of more traditional design issues; the Commission staff did not challenge substantial changes in the hotel's design features, such as the manner in which the hotel was terraced along the face of the bluff, and a significant increase in intensity of use from 300 to 398 hotel rooms in the final design.

A Few Basic Principles

Despite the widely varying physical, economic, and social characteristics of California's coastal areas, the preoccupation with preserving public views of the ocean and enhancing physical access to the coast has served as a leitmotiv of design review at the Coastal Commission level. The need to ensure use and enjoyment of the oceanfront define the basic principles of coastal design review, almost to the exclusion of more traditional concerns of design review, such as architectural form and style. In other words, coastal design review focuses almost totally on site planning rather than building form. Even in historic communities such as Monterey, the scale of structures in juxtaposition with historic structures (such as the historic adobes in Monterey) rather than the architectural style of the subject was the focus of design review.

In many areas of the country, the principle of public access to the coast has succumbed to the land values of waterfront locations for exclusively private development. If public access is treated merely as a legal requirement, which can be satisfied by providing an uninviting walkway that winds through an intimidatingly large project, then the concept of public access has no impact in the design review process. However, if one of the goals of coastal regulation is to "maximize public access to and along the coast," the preservation of visual and physical access becomes *the* basic principle of project site planning. Coastal design review then becomes a matter of assuring that:

1. public access is a central feature of all major projects;

2. major public views of the coast are precisely defined and protected through specific project development standards;

3. public use areas are made inviting in terms of size and location and private structures are set back from public areas to avoid any sense that public uses intrude on private areas; and

4. new access areas are linked with already existing or proposed public accessways to provide continuous walkways to and along the cost in areas buffered from vehicular intrusion.

The foregoing principles are not only consistent with an altruistic notion of the public good, they are also grounded in sound economics. Maintaining the scale of the coastal amenities that attract visitors is a principle that has been applied assiduously in many areas of Europe. Visual and physical access to the coast are key features of tourism attraction in Greece and Yugoslavia and are also obvious ingredients in such major attractions as Ghirardelli Square in San Francisco. Anyone who has driven the Malibu coast north of Los Angeles has passed through an area with the physical amenities and topography to rival the famous resorts of the Mediterranean. Unfortunately, private development prior to the passage of the Coastal Act created a visual and physical wall that effectively obliterated an amenity capable of providing a continuing source of tourism revenue to local governments and to the state and nation.

We have reviewed several redevelopment projects, including a number whose earlier plans were drastically revised in the course of coastal design regulation. And yet each of these projects has been a success, in terms of meeting both redevelopment costs and the financial requirements of private developers. If properly conceived, the provision of visual and physical access can effectively convert a regulatory "problem" into a money-making amenity. ●

WILLIAM M. BOYD

WILLIAM M. BOYD

WILLIAM M. BOYD

Notes:

1. The one attempt by the California Supreme Court to deal with aesthetic regulation (Metromedia, Inc. *vs.* City of San Diego [1981] 453 U.S. 490) was overturned by the U.S. Supreme Court on First Amendment free speech grounds, rather than aesthetic regulation grounds, and justices held widely divergent opinions on the possible scope of such regulation.

2. One interesting development from the regulatory perspective is the failure of a number of projects even to resemble the architectural renderings. As a result, the regional commission for the Big Sur area began to require that the building profile for each project had to be constructed on-site to define the extent of view impact.

3. Early in the design process, the City of Monterey hired a program consultant to review the functional allocations of the Conference Center space. The original proposal called for a 500-seat forum theater, an auditorium, meeting spaces, offices, and services areas. On the recommendation of the program consultant, an 1,800-seat concert theater replaced the 500-seat forum theater, sharply escalating the scale of the facility. The City viewed this change with considerable enthusiasm. Gary Chalupsky, head of Monterey's Redevelopment Agency, noted, "It was an opportunity to leverage an economically oriented project to get a civic amenity that the City had wanted for years."

LIZA RIDDLE

LIZA RIDDLE

Visual and physical access to the coast are key features of tourism attraction in European resorts and are also obvious ingredients in such major attractions as Ghirardelli Square in San Francisco. The Yugoslavian resorts of Hvav (top, opposite page), Split (middle, opposite page), and Opatija (bottom, opposite page) offer extensive pedestrian walkways along the waterfront with successful commercial development behind. A similar situation exists in San Francisco, where the private commercial development of Ghirardelli Square overlooks the heavily-used Aquatic Park, developed by the City in the late 1920s. Also located on the Aquatic Park lagoon is a State historic maritime park (at left in photograph above) and a public fishing pier, from which this photograph was taken.

The Urban Edge

Coastal Regulation:
The Designer's Perspective

SALLY WOODBRIDGE

"The consciousness of men does not determine their existence; nor does their existence determine their consciousness. Between the human consciousness and the material existence stand communications and designs, patterns, and values which influence decisively such consciousness as they have. . . . The designer is the creator and critic of the physical frame of private and public life. He represents man as maker of his own milieu."

—C. Wright Mills[1]

"The scenic and visual qualities of coastal areas shall be considered and protected as a resource of public importance. Permitted development shall be sited and designed to protect views along the ocean and scenic coastal areas, to minimize the alteration of natural land forms, to be visually compatible with the character of surrounding areas, and, where feasible, to restore and enhance visual quality in visually degraded areas. New development in highly scenic areas, such as those designated in the California Coastline and Preservation and Recreation Plan prepared by the Department of Parks and Recreation and by local governments, shall be subordinate to the character of its setting."

—California Coastal Act[2]

The path to good design lies not merely in the creative talent of a designer, but in the care taken by designer and developer alike to insure that a project is conceived and executed with an awareness of the constraints imposed by regulation as well as natural forces. The regulations enforced by various commissions and agencies, together with the obvious social and economic forces, are as important to the design of a project as its aesthetic harmony with nature.

In 1972, California's voters approved a citizen-initiated referendum, Proposition 20, intended to protect the State's coastal resources. Proposition 20 led to establishment of the California Coastal Commission to plan for and regulate coastal development, and to the adoption of the Coastal Act of 1976 to guide the Commission and coastal communities in their coastal planning.

A familiar scenario: a developer, having acquired a piece of coastal property, designs a project program with the aid of an economic analysis. Although the developer does not work with form and materials, his composition of facts and figures is no less crucial to the architectural product. The developer then gives his program to several architectural firms to draw up according to their different perceptions of how to get the best scheme for the budget. Since the array of problems is susceptible to more than one solution, the architect may work up different schemes if the fee is adequate and if he is instructed to do so. Still, it is unlikely that more than one scheme will reach the State Coastal Commission in the approval process.

The first shopping center project reviewed by the Coastal Commission was Santa Monica Place, developed by The Rouse Company. In contrast with other Rouse projects, the Company had to deal with stringent requirements of a Coastal Act mandating public view access to the ocean.

Presumably the developer is neither so inexperienced nor so uninformed that he would ignore the provisions of the Coastal Act (or, for that matter, any other regulations governing development projects) in preparing his program. But the criteria specified in the Coastal Act are admittedly open to interpretation. If the architects have not been briefed by the regulators themselves, they may not have heard all the messages or know all the options. Consequently their designs may not adequately address all the issues, and a permit denial may be the result. Because architects' and developers' egos are entangled in their projects—with such an investment of time and money it cannot be otherwise—they are aggrieved when their proposals are denied approval, and an adversary atmosphere may be established.

The strongest regulatory efforts of the Commission have been directed toward maximizing public access to the coast and minimizing the visual intrusion of buildings on the coastal landscape by reducing bulk and/or altering materials and color. Although these measures may redress the more egregious conflicts between man's handiwork and nature, the designers' creative energies are not directed to explore paths that lead to high quality design—the Coastal Act's constraints do not dictate aesthetics, nor could they. Certainly, within the constraints imposed by man and nature, an unimaginative designer/developer can take the scheme that didn't get built in Kansas City, squash it down or break it up, paint it brown or re-side it with redwood, and make it "coastal."

Nevertheless, the existence of a contemporary coastal vernacular building style, heavily dependent on the early Sea Ranch condominium and houses by Charles Moore and William Turnbull, testifies to the eagerness of designers, builders, and buyers for "approved" models. What good models exist? A survey of the recognized architectural gems on the coast does not reveal many that are directly useful today. The most acclaimed survivors from the past development of the coast are the Hotel Del Coronado in San Diego, Hearst's Castle in San Simeon, and the Carson House in Eureka. The splendid immodesty of these buildings bespeaks an age when the consensus was that human works should stand up against nature. Two outstanding examples from the recent past, the Nepenthe restaurant in Big Sur and the original demonstration housing cluster at Sea Ranch, represent the present consensus that human works should be in harmony with natural surroundings. Still, this visual consistency, though laudable, should not be automatically equated with high quality.

Given the entrenched perception of the regulatory process as an adversarial situation for the designer as well as the developer, battle fatigue, not art, is the most reasonable expectation. But optimism is a necessary ingredient of a vital design process. It behooves all who are concerned with preserving this fragile environment, while enhancing our enjoyment of it, to exert ourselves to find ways of improving design quality, not just getting the necessary permit approvals.

Within the system of priorities established by the Coastal Act—protection of views and open space, provision of access, and preservation of the natural environment—a variety of design approaches is possible. Although the empirical nature of the design process makes it impossible to generalize from one case to the next, still it is instructive to look at what has been built on the California coast during the last decade. The case studies which follow give depth to the issue of design and the regulatory process.

The Monterey Conference Center–A Question of Scale

The history of the Monterey Conference Center goes back over two decades. The main elements of the tale—major program changes, shifts in policy and personnel, rising costs, reduced expectations, disappointed hopes, growing community polarization, public education—all are factors affecting long-term public projects that become the focus of community attention. Invariably, those who bear the burden of proof for the project's success become embattled, and righteous zeal colors the actions of all parties.

A shortened version of the conference center story is presented here because it was one of the first battles fought before the Commission over the issues of appropriate height and bulk in an historic coastal setting, and because designers were some of the principal actors.

A model of the Monterey Conference Center demonstrates its scale and relationship to its surroundings.

The Monterey Conference Center opened in 1977, over twenty years after the site (about 45 acres of downtown between Del Monte Avenue and the waterfront) had been designated an official Urban Renewal Area. The first actions taken in the so-called Custom House Redevelopment Project made important changes in the area. By the late 1960s, almost all buildings except those certified as historic were cleared from around the Custom House; the part of Lighthouse Avenue that cut diagonally across the site was converted to an underground tunnel to remove vehicular traffic from the site. Above ground, the Custom House Plaza was created to provide a setting for the one- and two-story adobes, spaced now much as they had been in the 1850s. Through the auspices of the Redevelopment Agency, the plaza became a state park.

For the remaining acreage of the site, a land use marketability study had indicated a need for a downtown regional shopping center. J.C. Penney was to be the anchor store. Until 1970, the City marked time while developers came and went, but the site remained a desert. Meanwhile, the Del Monte Shopping Center was built on the edge of town with Macy's as the anchor store. In 1970 J.C. Penney dropped out of the downtown center scheme, and the whole concept collapsed.

In 1971, a change in the law permitted the City of Monterey to absorb the Redevelopment Agency into its own structure. Another feasibility study pointed to a convention center as the strongest development option for the vacant land. In 1972, a new staff headed by Gary Chalupsky took over the task of administering what was then called the Downtown/ Waterfront Redevelopment Project. An earlier general Urban Design Plan, commissioned by the City from a coalition of local architects (Hall & Goodhue, William D. Concolino & Associates, Wallace Holms & Associates, and Will Shaw & Associates), was adopted for use in developing design guidelines.

One of the most important aspects of the City of Monterey's new Conference Center project is the provision of a pedestrian plaza and accessway linking the downtown with the historic waterfront.

The City Redevelopment Agency then requested proposals from architectural firms to develop a master plan for the seven-acre parcel between Del Monte and the Custom House Plaza. This space was to contain a 300-room hotel, a conference center, and parking facilities with some commercial development and public open space. In 1973, Van Bourg/ Nakamura and Associates became the project architects for the conference center. The hotel developer, the Custom House Hotel Company, had the Kansas City firm, Kivett/Myers, as its architects. The conference center went ahead first. In the meantime, Chalupsky engaged the services of Will Shaw as review architect for the Urban Design Plan. Both Shaw and Van Bourg/Nakamura worked on the orientation, positioning, and massing of the hotel in relation to the conference center. In establishing the scale of the proposed development, the dual goals of perpetuating the image of the nineteenth century waterfront village and boosting that of the declining downtown area were deemed incompatible. To those who envisioned the project from downtown, the new rise of the buildings symbolized growth and optimism; for those who cared about tradition and the natural setting, the image was disastrous.

Early in the design process, the City hired a program consultant to review the functional allocations of the conference center space. The existing proposal called for a 500-seat forum theater, an auditorium, meeting spaces, offices, and services areas. On the recommendation of the program consultant, an 1,800-seat concert theater replaced the 500-seat forum theater, sharply escalating the scale of the facility. The City viewed this change with considerable enthusiasm. "It was," as Chalupsky put it, "an opportunity to leverage an economically oriented project to get a civic amenity that the City had wanted for years." Coming from the Midwest where every small town had its civic theater/auditorium, Chalupsky had been astonished to find Monterey without such an amenity.

The architects proceeded to design the conference center and the City cultivated community interest and support. According to Chalupsky, the City never argued that a full-fledged theater was to be a modest element. The argument was that size was a reasonable tradeoff for a civic facility that was otherwise unobtainable in comparable locations. Architect Mitch Van Bourg recalled the impossibility of designing such a large facility to look small. Meanwhile the owner of the *Monterey Peninsula Herald,* Paul Block, published an editorial expressing concern that Radio City Music Hall was going to be built in old Monterey. Gradually, the theater became a cause celebre. Said Van Bourg, "It had become a crusade, a labor of love. We just went overboard; had models built, and so on—we never made any money on that job."

Zealous opponents of the theater included other members of the architectural community, such as Hall & Goodhue of the original Urban Design team, and members of the Monterey History and Art Association. Nat Owings, the principal in the firm of Skidmore, Owings & Merrill and a resident of Big Sur, joined forces with this group. But the City, having secured the approval of the original plans by the Central Coast Regional Commission, was reasonably optimistic that the project would go ahead as planned.

In 1973, the Regional Commission's decision was appealed by Donald Goodhue, Mrs. C. Tod Singleton, and Mrs. Talcott Bates. The State Coastal Commission then heard the appeal and reviewed the project. Following the City's presentation, a set of speakers presented the opposition. The most effective of them was Nat Owings. Owings showed slides of the conference center site taken from all the sensitive view points around it, projected onto the featureless profile of the proposed center. This dramatically illustrated the vistas that would be cropped because of the center's height. The most offending structure was the theater fly loft, which rose to a height only three feet shorter than the San Carlos Hotel, downtown's tallest building.

This remarkable presentation carried the day. In effect, the Coastal Commission provided a forum where, in the course of public meetings, issues were defined and aired. As a result, the conference center was redesigned without the theater, and opened in 1977.

In retrospect we might ask why the City pursued a course that seems now so wrong-headed. Chalupsky said that all along he suspected the theater might prove to be an economic white elephant. But the City team also felt that the opposition was irrational. "Perhaps we stayed with it too long," Chalupsky said, "but you become religious about what you do. When the approval was reversed, we knew we still had a project and we went ahead." Neither Chalupsky nor Van Bourg denies that the project as finally redesigned and built is not an aesthetic improvement over what was turned down. According to Van Bourg, "Design is the intuitive product of problem solving. Growth and improvement often come from compromise. But no good architect can be comfortable with the wasted time and money and the erosion of design possibilities that accompanies delay. What was built was the most modest thing ever proposed for that site, but not because the money went directly into making it that way."

This is the recurring lament of architects who work within regulatory / review processes. The stop-and-go and return-to-go aspects are hard on egos as well as budgets. "The process is faulty," says Van Bourg, "in the same way that mountainsides are faulty. You think you're climbing up and suddenly you're down a hole."

From the Commissions's viewpoint, however, the regulatory process achieved the only accommodation possible at that late date by reducing the size of the facility.

Santa Monica Place–A Point of View

The first shopping center reviewed by the Coastal Commission was Santa Monica Place, a development of The Rouse Company with Frank O. Gehry & Associates as architects. The center occupies two square blocks bounded north-south by Colorado and Broadway and east-west by Second and Fourth Streets; it is a piece of a nine-acre redevelopment area just a short city block from the ocean. To the north is Santa Monica Mall, the 1920s shopping district converted into a pedestrian mall during the first phase of the city's redevelopment plan. To the south is a Sears department store. The west end of the center faces toward the beach and the Municipal Pier, completed in 1921 and a landmark from the hey-day of the seaside community.

The proposed height of the complex was originally 112 feet. When it opened in 1981, the complex was 85 feet high, but it

still dominated its surroundings. With 163 shops, two department stores, and two six-story parking garages around an enclosed, all-weather mall, the density of use is far greater than anything else in the area. Yet, thanks to the designer's sensitivity, Santa Monica Place is not a monolithic fortress, but rather an aggregation of separate parts, each considered in relation to the adjacent area. Visually, the center brings the kind of excitement and festiveness to the area that compensates for the jump in scale over its neighbors.

Since Gehry's commission required his participation in the approval process, the architect met with the Regional Coastal Commission early in the design process. The Regional Commission's concerns focused on energy conservation, which in this locale meant reducing the cooling loads for the complex. Since the lighting and air conditioning loads are significantly higher for an enclosed mall, the regulators argued for an open mall with natural ventilation for the stores. Even though the seaside micro-climate was favorable for such a concept, it proved impossible to persuade the developer and department store investors to depart from the current suburban model. To rule against air conditioning amounted to a project denial.

Regional approval of the proposed design did not, however, mean clear sailing for the project. Members of the community opposed the scale of the complex and saw it as a harbinger of even larger scale development that would permanently alter the existing community. This group organized in opposition and appealed the regional approval to the State Coastal Commission.

With the involvement of the State Commission staff, new issues appeared on the bargaining table. Height was one; the view corridor to the ocean was another. The height of the complex was reduced by 27 feet to make the center more compatible with the old Santa Monica Mall.

The most radical change was the redesign of the west end to acknowledge the ocean view. In response to the State Coastal Commission staff recommendation that a minimum of 10,000 square feet of space be devoted to public use as restaurants, open decks, etc. on the second and third levels of the mall's west side, and that adjacent leasable space have direct access to this outside area, the architects designed a system of decks with a structural aesthetic that alludes to things nautical, specifically to the Municipal Pier.

When asked how he felt about having to redesign parts of the project, Gehry said he welcomed the opportunity to make changes that he felt were an improvement. Since even enlightened developers, such as the Rouse Corporation, do not usually provide public amenities unrelated to commercial opportunities unless required to do so, it is unlikely that architects

A major Coastal Commission requirement of the Rouse Company's Santa Monica Place project was a set of viewing platforms providing public views of the ocean. The original plan had no such provision, effectively walling off the ocean from visitors.

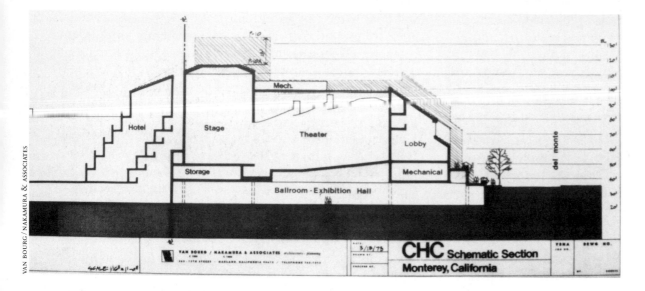

VAN BOURG / NAKAMURA & ASSOCIATES

CHC Schematic Section
Monterey, California

The Coastal Commission considered the original design of the Monterey Conference Center (shown at left and opposite above) to be out of scale with surrounding historic and other structures. The bulk and scale of the Center as finally built (pictured at bottom on the opposite page) were significantly reduced to harmonize with the redesign of the surrounding area.

will be able to initiate them. In this case, the improvement of the design was the result of an appeal that shifted the approval process from the local to the state level.

Commenting on the designer's role in the regulatory process, Gehry said:

"By and large, when the architect can sit down with an informed and sympathetic bureaucrat, the mechanism starts to work to improve the project. The bureaucracy should not look at the designer—who most of the time is an idealist—as the adversary. If the regulators want quality design, they should have more say about who the designers are. By now there are people around with good track records who should be given first consideration. If the developers don't know who they are, there should be ways of finding out. I realize that kind of thing appears elitist, but if the goal is important, the means should correspond to it."

Conclusion

Buildings do not spring directly from architect's plans. Rather they result from the multiple actions of people and of social and economic forces. As these case studies show, the continuous reformulation of problems put under the heading "design program" requires great flexibility. Yet there is a tendency to try for a product before the program is fully formulated. Though understandable from the point of view of the designer who trades in the visual translations of verbal constructs, this tendency is potentially damaging to both process and product.

The foregoing case studies describe design modifications resulting from the combination of regulatory, economic, and

social forces. In the case of the Monterey Conference Center, building size was reduced to make the project compatible with its surroundings. The debate over the proposed center polarized the community, a situation that could have been avoided by early communication among all factions to achieve a consensus.

In the case of Santa Monica Place, intervention by the Coastal Commission required the designer to recognize the coastal setting of the project. Builders of shopping centers want to focus the visitor's entire attention on the consumption of commodities, not on open air vistas. The proposed design for this shopping center did not hint at its proximity to the sea; redesign provided public recreational opportunities and integrated the building with the coastal environment. The completed project is an award-winning design widely acknowledged for its public amenities and a commercially successful enterprise.

These considerations do not guarantee that each coastal project will be an architectural wonder. Within the framework established by the Coastal Act and the Commission, the design is the domain of the architect. And the architect, like anyone else, is susceptible to the strains of battle fatigue in a prolonged regulatory debate.

Though many designers view regulation as a hindrance, coastal protection is a reality. This reality obligates designers to become aware of regulatory concerns, to adapt to these concerns, and to communicate them to their clients. ●

Notes:

1. C. Wright Mills, "Man in the Middle: The Designer," in *Power, Politics and People;* collected essays of C. Wright Mills, edited by Irving Louis Horovitz (New York: Oxford University Press, 1963).

2. California Coastal Act, Public Resources Code, Section 30251.

The Urban Edge

Urban Waterfront Restoration on the California Coast

GRAY BRECHIN

Robinson Jeffers' Hawk Tower rises from the granite tor on Carmel Bay like a projection of its basement rock, a wedding of human design and nature that is an embodiment of the poet's thought. From its parapet, Jeffers watched the California coast fill with one of the greatest migrations in history. As he saw Carmel itself become a parody of its bohemian legend and his own trees felled for encroaching houses, he sought solace in the volley of surf at the foot of his tower and the geological perspectives that it suggested. Witnessing what he called the coming of the spoiler, he anticipated the imminent "bath of a storm that prepares up the long coast of the future" and found his own comfort in "the fountains of the boiling stars, the flowers on the foreland, the ever-returning roses of dawn."

The spoilation which Jeffers regretted was anticipated earlier by Frederick Law Olmsted. While San Francisco Bay struck him in 1862 as "the noblest possible," the city beside it seemed a jerry-built tinder box. What he observed of San Francisco in 1865 applied to California land use in general: "Worthy to be, and destined to be one of the largest . . . cities in the world, it must at some time escape from the influences that happen to be associated with the discovery of gold in California."

Olmsted clearly saw that the short-sighted rapacity that ravaged the Sierra foothills and Central Valley left its imprint on cities as well. Nowhere is this more indelibly evident than in San Francisco where, responding more to the abstractions of the marketplace than the realities of topography, a grid pattern of streets appropriate to Kansas was laid on the city's precipitous hills. Indeed, the mining mentality that gave romantic birth to the state established one of California's

most tenacious traditions. California has, since the Gold Rush, been a land of nomads living all too lightly on their remarkable land. If they praise the land's beneficence, it has all too often been only to sell it.

Development of the populous coast and Bay has been dictated largely by speculation and industrial demand. In only a few instances—the 1915 World's Fair in San Francisco and the Golden Gate Bridge, for example—have thoughtful designs worthy of their sites appeared. So thoughtless was the treatment of San Francisco Bay that, as early as 1918, architect Irving Morrow (later to design the Golden Gate Bridge) could lament that "It can scarcely be maintained that the hand of man has been laid upon this scene with the same affection, not to speak of intelligence, that has usually characterized its activity in the old world."

It cannot be denied that California's superlative scenery and climate have led Californians to devise an unsurpassed system of county, state, and national parks as well as a seminal conservation movement thath now has worldwide impact. Yet spot reservations have proved inadequate and innovative mechanisms to regulate land use are demanded by the continuing abuse of the land. Traditional methods have proved insufficient: regional planning authorities have frequently proved toothless while urban redevelopment agencies have traditionally suffered from an excess of power in a limited area and an immunity to broad community concerns. Regulatory agencies, such as the Coastal Commission, are perceived as representing the clumsy and restraining hand of bureaucracy. However good the intent, the regulatory process is regarded as time-consuming and reactive, its decrees as frequently harsh and arbitrary.

East Brother Light Station in San Francisco Bay (left) and Robinson Jeffers' Tor House on Carmel Bay (above and right) successfully integrate design with their natural sites.

Recently, attempts have been made to promote sound, environmentally sensitive design through positive action rather than reactive regulation. In numerous coastal cities, public agencies have taken the lead in restoring waterfronts by providing site improvements and public amenities and by working out collaborative arrangements with the private sector. Many of these efforts have deliberately sought to improve or reclaim public access to the urban shoreline through appropriate design. This kind of direct public action has become increasingly necessary. Public investment is needed to attract private investment to the waterfront area. The high costs of waterfront redevelopment also necessitate public investment and intervention to ensure that redevelopment plans include facilities for public use of the waterfront.

Through the regulatory process on the California coast, the Coastal Commission has forced permit applicants to consider the demands of a coastal location. Our first example of positive public action, the San Francisco Bay Conservation and Development Commission's work in stimulating preparation of a plan for San Francisco's waterfront, shows how the constructive use of regulatory and planning powers can be taken one step further. The Bay Conservation and Development Commission (BCDC) is the regulatory agency responsible for San Francisco Bay. After initial denial of a waterfront plan as inconsistent with the San Francisco Bay Plan's environmental goals, BCDC embarked on a collaborative planning effort with the Port Commission, the Planning Department, and the

Redevelopment Agency, with substantial input from a citizen's advisory committee. The San Francisco Northeastern Waterfront Plan is the result.

Public agencies have also become directly involved in the creation of coastal design through project development. In California, the State Coastal Conservancy has used its broad authority to purchase, sell, and develop land to achieve environmental goals on the coast. In the second example that follows, the Conservancy worked to resolve complex land use and design conflicts involving local government, private landowners, prospective developers, citizen groups, and a host of public special-purpose agencies.

Northeastern Waterfront Plan for San Francisco

San Francisco's bayshore waterfront is a remarkable resource caught in the coils of a serpentine bureaucracy. Only recently have changes begun that could transform the area into one of the nation's great public amenities.

For nearly a century, San Francisco was the West Coast's leading port. Wooden finger piers fanning from its northeast shore accommodated countless freighters, passenger ships, and ferries while a palisade of monumental facades walled the city from the Bay and gave the Embarcadero a degree of stage-set grandeur. Backed by warehouses, markets, downtown, and hillside residential areas, the waterfront was perhaps the city's most colorful and active area.

San Francisco's northeastern water-front area, shown opposite below, is characterized by wooden finger piers overlooked by the historic Coit Tower and the modern skyscrapers of the financial district. The Levi Strauss Company's Levi Plaza development (right), located between Coit Tower and the Embarcadero piers, attempts to harmonize with this diverse urban waterfront setting.

LEVI STRAUSS & CO.

Technological changes (e.g., the introduction of containerized vessels), the abandonment of the ferries, decline in passenger travel, and mismanagement resulted in the port's steady decline following World War II. The construction of the Embarcadero Freeway and the obliteration of the produce market for the Golden Gate Redevelopment Project contributed to the area's atrophy and alienation. Once one of the City's most vital neighborhoods, it rapidly became one of its most neglected.

Port Commissioner Cyril Magnin's 1959 plan for an "Embarcadero City" envisioned a revitalized waterfront and is a reminder of that megalomaniacal era of urban design. Embarcadero City simply abolished the old port north of the Ferry Building and converted it to non-maritime commercial uses requiring a good deal of bay fill. While never realized, the scheme led to the highly-charged battle over U.S. Steel's plans to erect a 550-foot high-rise on the waterfront south of the Ferry Building. While that plan was squashed mainly by action of the regional BCDC, the controversy it engendered was largely responsible for the formulation of a Northeastern Waterfront Plan, issued by the Department of City Planning in 1980, that is significantly different from the earlier Embarcadero City proposal.

San Francisco's waterfront represents a maze of overlapping and frequently competing jurisdictions primarily represented by the BCDC, CalTrans, San Francisco Port Commission, the Planning Commission, and the Redevelopment Agency. The process of developing a plan for the waterfront has been Byzantine in its complexity and glacial in its progress, but several aspects of it are significant. An advisory committee with citizen participation helped formulate the plan instead of the previously delivered plan-by-fiat. And, responding to growing preservationist sentiment, the architectural firm of ROMA commissioned a survey of the outstanding historical resources worthy of preservation in the study area. Among these are a number of nineteenth century brick warehouses which had escaped the 1906 fire.

The resulting plan divides the waterfront into four sub-areas and develops a multi-use program rich in public, bay-oriented amenities, and maritime uses, as well as commercial development. As the plan itself states, it reflects not simply "what is possible, but rather what is desirable from the broadest public interest point of view." It recommends policies that "contribute to the waterfront's environmental quality, enhance the economic vitality of the Port and the City, preserve the unique maritime character, and provide for the maximum feasible visual and physical access to and along the Bay."

Construction is already under way on a pedestrian promenade south of the Ferry Building that has resulted in the demolition of decayed piers and sheds and the opening of views of the Bay Bridge. A projected restoration and reuse of the mutilated Ferry Building by the firm of I.M. Pei echoes similar and successful projects in Boston and Baltimore. The privately-developed Levi Plaza, incorporating a handsomely initially concluded that the proposed center failed not only to meet provisions of the Act but was probably too large to be economically viable.

Then in July 1979, the Conservancy approved $35,000 for the development of an urban waterfront restoration program. Working with the staffs of the regional and state Coastal Commissions, a citizens' advisory committee for the City of Eureka, and the San Francisco architectural firm of Jericho Alpha, the Conservancy helped to formulate a plan which meets the criteria of the Coastal Act and has been incorporated into the Eureka Local Coastal Program.

The revised Eureka plan emphasized mixed-use development with a strong emphasis on public amenities and access, which were stressed by the Conservancy. Fronting on the harbor and tied to the Old Town redevelopment area by two pedestrian footbridges, the revamped waterfront would be flanked to the east and west by two parks of about an acre each. The parks provide direct access to Humboldt Bay and are connected by a 1,700-foot promenade. A two-part community conference center, smaller than the original proposal and totally redesigned, is located in the center of the project site. This facility would consist of a flexible, 3,500-seat auditorium adjacent to a multi-purpose "Victorian Galleria" intended for exhibits, banquets, recreation, and meeting rooms. Furthermore, a public amphitheater in East Park would provide space for *al fresco* performances as well as views of the harbor and docked historic ships.

The revised waterfront restoration program appears to meet the needs of the community and the provisions of the Coastal Act far better than the initial plans for a conference center. Not only are views of the Carson Mansion and the bay assured, but the reduced size of the center will increase the economic feasibility of the project. Instead of a single-purpose convention center to accommodate the tourist trade, the structure, as envisioned, will be a genuine community center that can be used by Eureka residents, many of whom, especially elderly and low- to moderate-income individuals, live in adjoining neighborhoods. The design considerately integrates the city and its waterfront by removing the present palisade of deteriorated and vacant structures and knitting the complex to the Old Town with pedestrian bridges, as well as creating a marine promenade.

Conclusion

Under the umbrella of the Coastal Act, the State's coastal cities have attempted to stimulate and guide coastal development and use within their jurisdictions. The Coastal Commission's regulation of coastal land use has frequently proved inadequate in resolving land use disputes and in encouraging effective restoration for degraded urban and natural environments.

The State Coastal Conservancy has demonstrated that a state agency can act as mediator and facilitator in the resolution of complex land use problems. And even more significantly, we have seen that communities can snatch consensus from the jaws of dissension and cities can develop economically feasible projects that maximize public amenities while creating opportunities for needed private investment.

On the San Francisco waterfront, the production of a coordinated multi-use design has demonstrated that a regulatory agency, in this instance, the BCDC, can stimulate creative design solutions—as well as inhibit development—through the threat of imposed constraints. ●

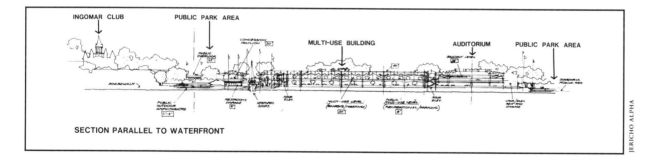

INGOMAR CLUB   PUBLIC PARK AREA   MULTI-USE BUILDING   AUDITORIUM   PUBLIC PARK AREA

SECTION PARALLEL TO WATERFRONT

JERICHO ALPHA

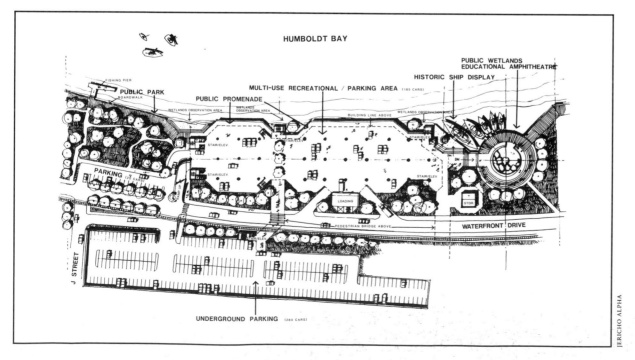

HUMBOLDT BAY

PUBLIC WETLANDS EDUCATIONAL AMPHITHEATRE

HISTORIC SHIP DISPLAY

FISHING PIER

PUBLIC PARK
BOARDWALK

MULTI-USE RECREATIONAL / PARKING AREA (185 CARS)

PUBLIC PROMENADE

PARKING

LOADING

PEDESTRIAN BRIDGE ABOVE

WATERFRONT DRIVE

J STREET

UNDERGROUND PARKING (280 CARS)

JERICHO ALPHA

The Carson House in Eureka, a Victorian structure which has been carefully preserved in pristine condition, overlooks the site of one of the City's major waterfront restoration projects (seen in plan on opposite page), which is being implemented with the assistance of the State Coastal Conservancy. Eureka's waterfront is characterized by a mix of fishing and industrial uses (below) as well as dilapidated areas.

development adequate to restore and sustain the wharf economically has a high price tag in congestion and commercialism.

The City estimated the cost of restoration to be about $3 million; the City had about $1 million available for the project. The Conservancy's first step was to investigate alternate methods of funding restoration that would allow a lower density of development. The agency staff found what they were looking for. The Federal Coastal Energy Impact Program's (CEIP) loan program contributed $1.4 million, to be repaid over a 30-year period. The Conservancy contributed $400,000, half to be paid back within ten years from pier revenues. A grant for the remaining $200,000 was to be made by the Wildlife Conservation Board, another state agency.

The City's new plan called for commercial development roughly equivalent to the amount existing before the fire. Projections indicated that revenues from this development could cover continuing operation and maintenance costs, which included debt service on the CEIP construction loan.

Behind this sparse account is a long series of discussions, meetings, and correspondence with city staff, Commission staff, local environmentalists, and federal and state funding agency personnel. The Conservancy staff worked to elicit concerns and requirements, seek opportunities for accommodation, and identify limits. The key element in the accommodation was establishment of a level of feasible development that could be financially self-supporting yet remain consistent with Coastal Act policies concerning access, preservation of views, and priority uses (in this case, public recreation). In the completed project, roughly three-fourths of the deck area remain open public space for fishing, strolling, and viewing the sights. The buildings on the pier are limited in bulk and location as well as total floor area; public recreation and access are accorded priority over other uses and activities on the pier.

The actual design of the buildings, which include a large restaurant, a coffee shop, a fish market and bait shop, and several other stores, was left to the city's architects. The architects worked within the pier's overall design "envelope" as allocated in the plan. A design competition, suggested by the Conservancy, was ruled out by the City in the interests of rapid completion of the project.

Appropriate Development in Rural Areas: Whiskey Shoals

Subdivisions created on coastal lands before 1972 pose a serious land use problem. Areas which are inappropriate for any development have been divided into many small lots. Protection of the coast—its views, open space, and shoreline—requires preventing development on these lots.

The Coastal Commission's denial of building permits for many such lots has meant years of delay, uncertainty, and hardship for the individuals who own the land. The 65-acre Whiskey Shoals subdivision along the Mendocino County coast in northern California is one such instance.

Before 1972, Whiskey Shoals was subdivided into 72 lots for single-family dwellings. The developer built an access road, installed water lines and utilities, and sold 21 of the lots before the Coastal Commission put a moratorium on building. No houses had been built at the time of the moratorium. If building had proceeded as planned, houses would have dotted the landscape between Highway 1 and the sea, cut off access to the shore from the road, and permanently changed the landscape of coastal beaches, natural grassland, and Bishop pine.

Between 1972 and 1978, two Whiskey Shoals landowners submitted permit applications to the Coastal Commission; both were denied. The Commission requested Conservancy assistance in resolving this land use conflict. How could this

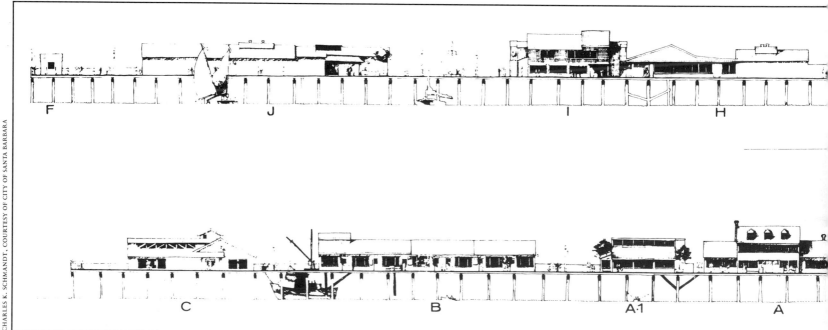

The design for the restoration of Santa Barbara's Stearn's Wharf (below), which was finally approved by both the City and the Coastal Commission, called for restoring roughly the same amount of developed commercial space as previously existed, while leaving about three-fourths of the pier's deck area free for public use. The illustrations above and left highlight the pier's major commercial use, a large restaurant on the site of the former Harbor Restaurant.

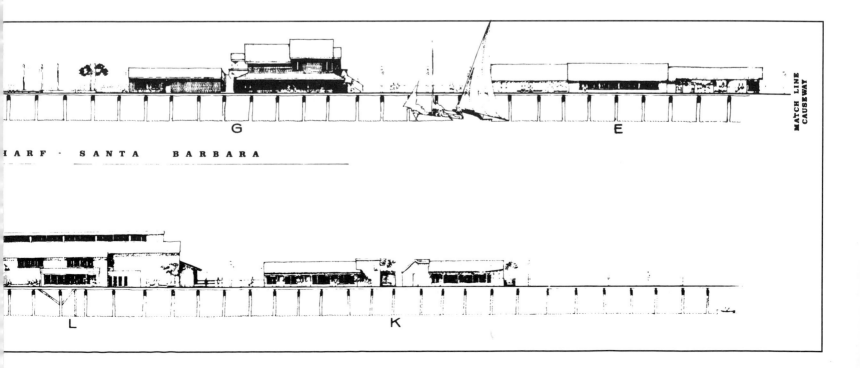

HARF · SANTA BARBARA

Participation for Accommodation: Oceanside

Urban waterfront restoration, by its complex nature, generates situations in which creative development is not only appropriate, but quite probably the only way to ensure that coastal resources in the urban setting can be protected and restored. A good case in point comes from the northern San Diego County City of Oceanside, located next to Camp Pendleton. The Conservancy again was asked to help, this time to plan the restoration of some public recreational facilities on the city's deteriorated Strand beachfront.

Oceanside had seen better days as a southern California beach resort, and its badly eroded beach symbolized its overall economic decline. In reconciling local and state needs regarding public access, the project scope was expanded to include restoration of one and one-fourth miles of urban beachfront.

The restoration program was prepared by participating citizens in a public community design workshop process. Participants walked the site, developed design guidelines for the project, helped select a consulting design team through a two-day public competition, then worked with the winning design group, a consulting economist, and City and Conservancy staff to prepare the restoration plan. The initial workshop included improvements to a municipal pier, community center and ampitheatre, acquisition of several acres of private land for new shorefront public parks, plus other improvements.

The workshops were under way when a new controversy flared. At a public hearing, citizens discovered that while the workshops were proceeding, a private developer under contract to the city redevelopment agency was busy preparing a master redevelopment plan for the entire downtown including the Strand beachfront, without benefit of public input. The ensuing outcry led the City to have the developer's representative attend the community workshops to discuss with the citizens points of disagreement between the two plans. Six main issues surfaced. Subsequent discussions between the parties quickly resolved five of the points. The sixth, disagreement over whether a particular site should be used for a public park or for condominiums, led to a mutually acceptable solution, which was incorporated into the final restoration plan. This plan was endorsed by the workshop participants, the City Council, the Conservancy, and Coastal Commission, and was acceptable to the developer. The plan is now being carried out by the City, assisted by a citizens' task force formed from workshop participants.

Here, again, communication among the concerned parties aimed at reaching a mutually agreeable solution without detriment to the beachfront resource, and eventually led to accommodation and action. The final plan maintained the amount of open space and access determined in the workshops. It contained a variety of public and commercial improvements that are expected to help stimulate the city's revival, and restore the Strand to some of its former attractiveness.

Conclusion

The three projects cited exemplify unique, non-confrontational attempts to resolve difficult coastal resource dilemmas. In each case, regulatory methods alone were inadequate. The solutions each reflected a deliberate attempt to preserve the resource—a pier, views, a beachfront—intact through compatible design. They were also tailored to their own specific situations, as with the use of a CEIP loan for Stearns Wharf or the Oceanside design workshops and competition, and the Conservancy worked closely with those involved locally in each project. Above all, these solutions were evolved through a process of mediation, avoiding the pitfalls of an adversarial proceeding. It is this process, rather than any particular solution, that has broad applicability. If the Conservancy's experience is any indication, such an approach can provide government with a more supportive, yet more economical role in a variety of contexts. Accommodation is cheaper than litigation.

The seeking of accommodation among diverse interests to resolve land use and design conflicts can be effective in a variety of circumstances. And if current rising prices and tight budgets continue, the need for accommodation will be even more evident. The public sector will be even less able to make large purchases of coastal lands for preservation and restoration purposes.

Creative development provides an alternative approach toward resource preservation. The Conservancy's projects—and creative development projects elsewhere in the country—can serve as models of land use planning through positive governmental action. If the nation's resource lands are to be protected, this is a process that must be given careful consideration. ●

Notes:

1. California State Coastal Conservancy Act, Public Resources Code, Section 31203.
2. Robert A. Lemire, *Creative Land Development: Bridge to the Future,* (Boston: Houghton Mifflin Company, 1979).

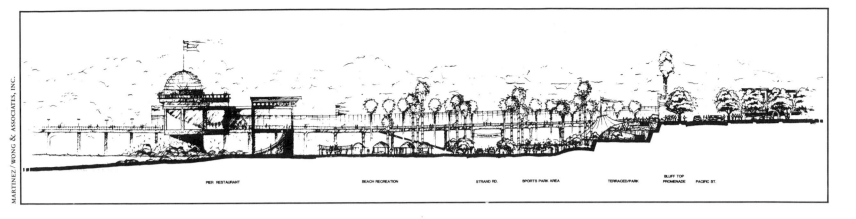

PIER RESTAURANT   BEACH RECREATION   STRAND RD.   SPORTS PARK AREA   TERRACED/PARK   BLUFF TOP PROMENADE   PACIFIC ST.

STRAND OPEN 10 10/45

6TH STREET BEACH DROP OFF

The restoration plan for the City of Occanside's Strand waterfront was the result of a series of community workshops that included a design competition to select the consulting designer/architect. The winning design (a major feature of which is shown at top) was submitted by the San Diego firm of Martinez/Wong & Associates, Inc. Among the strong competitors were the designs of Moore, Ruble and Yudell (center) and Wallace, Roberts and Todd (bottom). The perspective shown at left was executed by Ron Yeo and Associates and Lang and Wood, who acted as design consultants to the city in implementing the project. This is the first known instance of state government working with citizens through this innovative means to arrive at a design solution to a complex land use problem.

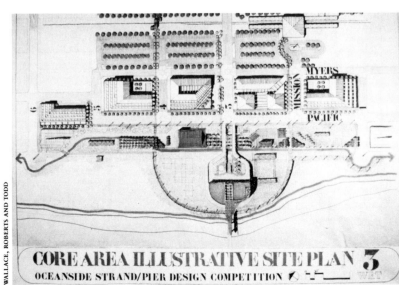

CORE AREA ILLUSTRATIVE SITE PLAN 3
OCEANSIDE STRAND/PIER DESIGN COMPETITION

The Urban Edge

Citizen Participation and Responsibility: Involving the Community in Planning and Design

PETER S. BRAND

Corks popped; glasses clinked; and champagne flowed. At a champagne gala open to the entire community, the City of Seal Beach was celebrating the completion of a $12 million redevelopment plan—created and designed by the citizens of Seal Beach.

The celebration was the conclusion of a five-month experiment in community action and participation. The planning process had started with two hundred and fifty citizens—all the people whom planning consultants could coax into a series of workshops. Working with internationally known architect Charles Moore and a team of consultants, these citizens had planned and obtained approval for a major change in their city: the restoration of a nine-acre coastal site for public use with a development that would provide a seven-acre park and cultural center, yet would not be an economic burden to the city.

The citizens came to the workshops with a limited knowledge of planning, design, and economic feasibility. They left knowing how to organize and carry through a significant environmental improvement in their community. The story of the Seal Beach project is one of the more remarkable tales of the revolution in land use control on the California coast.

Battle of the Beach

On a wide sandy beach overlooking the San Gabriel River, nine acres of land lay unused, fenced, surrounded by development, and empty except for the remnants of an old power plant. The Los Angeles Department of Water and Power (DWP), a large and powerful city agency, had abandoned the site and demolished the existing power plant, but had never sold the land, instead holding it in its vacant state.

This site was in the City of Seal Beach, a community of 27,000 people located in the belt of urban sprawl that stretches south from Long Beach in Los Angeles County to Newport Beach in Orange County. Beach land is a prime commodity in this area, and coastal land values frequently rise to $500,000 per acre. Consequently, the empty parcel of land was eyed by developers as a site for more houses, coveted by the citizens as a park, seen by city administrators as a source of revenue, and ultimately became the subject of a heated battle for control.

With the passage of California's Coastal Initiative (Proposition 20) in 1972, the site came under the regulatory control of the California Coastal Commission. Over a period of years, developers approached the Commission with proposals for the site, but the Commission wanted the land preserved for public use as a park, if there was to be any development at all.

In 1977, a proposal to build homes on the land, filling the site and leaving only slivers of open space around the edges, stirred up local controversy. The Coastal Commission still wanted a park. A vocal group of Seal Beach residents also wanted the land saved in open space. Other local interests wanted the city to profit by developing the site. The developer wanted to build condominiums. But a single coastal site cannot be all things to all people, and the dispute raged over the best use of the land. In 1978, at the urging of citizens, the city sought the aid of the State Coastal Conservancy, a state agency created to assist in the resolution of coastal land use conflicts.

The Conservancy joined the fray—not as a combatant, but as a mediator and facilitator. The most obvious remedy—purchase of the land by the Conservancy or another public

Workshop # 1: Make a Wish
At the first workshop, held in December 1977, Jim Burns asked everyone to write a postcard to Santa stating their expectations from the community planning process and their Christmas gift wish for the site. The simple task transformed the audience into active participants.

Workshop # 2: Build a Dream
In the late afternoon, participants worked in groups to devise their own three-dimensional visions of the project, using blank paper, scissors, crayons, parsley for trees, and Fruit Loops. The architects acted as facilitators while each group argued, agreed, pasted up their plan and proudly presented it to the rest of the workshop.

Workshop # 3: Make a Model
Architects Moore, Ruble, and Yudell responded at the next workshop with a model that synthesized ideas from the workshop consensus into a "kit of parts," containing buildings and site uses that the citizens could manipulate and rearrange.

Workshop # 4: Complete a Workable Plan
At the last workshop, the architects presented the final conceptual plan synthesis, a detailed perspective to enable the workshop participants to visualize how their proposals might finally look.

entity—was not possible because of the very high price sought by DWP. Conservancy staff started with another approach: If people's expectations were more realistic, an alternate solution might be feasible. The Conservancy's Executive Officer, Joseph Petrillo, convinced the Seal Beach City Council to allow the agency to arrange for preparation of a "restoration plan," and the agency decided to try active community participation in planning and design, rather than the traditional means of consultant studies and public hearings. Resolving the conflict meant involving local citizens in open discussion of the problems and potentials of the site and a realistic assessment of economic constraints and community needs, including those of the larger regional community that uses Seal Beach's waterfront.

The Conservancy applied for and received a National Endowment for the Arts "City Options" grant under NEA's Architecture and Environmental Arts Program to conduct a community participation planning and design process. With this grant, the Conservancy hired a team of consultants: public involvement specialist and urban design consultant Jim Burns; architect Charles Moore and his partners, John Ruble and Buzz Yudell; and the economist for the architects, Leland Burns.

Citizen participation was not an idea originated by the Conservancy. For the past quarter of a century, planners have been experimenting with citizen participation; most recently, Lawrence Halprin, Jim Burns, and their associates created what they called the "Take Part Process" of citizen participation, which has been applied with some success on the West Coast.[1] The Conservancy sponsored a series of four public workshops utilizing many common planning techniques and a few innovations.

The plan that emerged from the workshops proposed public and private structures on thirty percent of the site with the remainder devoted to intensive park development. The plan called for the City to purchase, restore, and develop the site for public use, primarily with private revenues generated on site. Two restaurants and fourteen condominiums placed on the inland ten percent of the site were to provide revenues sufficient to pay for $5 million of the $6 million public cost, including acquisition, massive site restoration, nearly seven acres of park development, and a cultural center and hostel. The designs maximized public access throughout the site by keeping the condominiums above ground-floor shops at the rear of the site, leaving the riverside open and views unobstructed.

The citizens sought to make the project self-sufficient, and succeeded. The excess annual revenue stream from the river-front restaurants would pay for operation and maintenance of the park. Moreover, under expected rather than worst case commercial performance estimates, the restaurants and shops would provide a tidy and increasing surplus revenue fund to the city.

Within the five-month workshop series, the community succeeded in designing a public project that would serve the community at no cost to the city while providing a place attractive to millions of residents and visitors to Southern California. Following adoption of the restoration plan and design by the workshop participants, approvals were obtained successively from the Seal Beach City Council, the State Coastal Conservancy, and the California Coastal Commission.

Getting it Done

Implementation began immediately, spurred on and monitored by a citizen committee of workshop participants. Momentum was crucial to keep such a diversified and innovative project alive. A low-interest site-acquisition loan of $3.1 million was applied for from the Federal Coastal Energy Impact Program (CEIP); a grant of $450,000 was approved by Orange County, with matching funds to come from the Federal Heritage Conservation and Recreation Service (HCRS). But DWP took over a year to complete an appraisal and begin negotiations, and by that time (late in 1981) the Reagan administration rescinded the HCRS and CEIP programs that were to provide funds. The rescission was fought unsuccessfully.

With the loss of public funds, private capital became much more important. The possibility of losing the public quality of the community participation plan again arose. Hilton was ready to push through a proposal to put a 250-room hotel on the beachfront, and other private proposals were being considered. But the workshop participants, who had spent two years following various economic analyses of the project, believed they could keep development within the 30 percent envelope set aside and still get a public park on most of the site by eliminating the cultural center and hostel.

The citizen group made a counterproposal to the Council: Why not get all potential developers to submit their proposals at once, in the open? Council agreed, and at the subsequent meeting numerous developers showed schemes for hotels, family inns, and condominiums both luxury and affordable. Some schemes were spiced with various offers of parks, theater facilities, and hostel-type accommodations, responding to the citizen group's concerns. One developer gained special favor with a plan to include the seven-acre park and keep his

Final perspective sketches, such as the one shown opposite, helped the citizens to visualize how their site plans would actually look. In this design, the citizens incorporated commercial development to help pay for many of the public amenities provided.

family-oriented hotel at the other end of the site away from the beach.

Response by the developers convinced the Council to adopt the 30 percent requirement as permanent zoning for the site. Ardent advocate Barbara Rountree responded, "It's the only way we see how we are ever going to get the park and facilities we want." The San Gabriel Pacific Park Society, whose membership now includes old advocates and new believers in the project, continues to take responsibility for the recommendations conceived in the workshops; they have since incorporated as a non-profit foundation to assist in operation and maintenance of the site. Mrs. Rountree, president of the Society, states: "Our role now is stewardship."

For the citizen group, the project has evolved from their dream to a private developer's project with fewer public benefits. But the citizens are still involved—developers now come to them—and they understand what is happening. "The process has really turned the community around," says a resident who attended the workshops. "It has raised our consciousness, encouraged people to speak out, and has brought everything into the open the way it should."

Think Globally; Act Locally

The Seal Beach case shows that the strength and creativity of a community participation process can be sustained even in the most difficult circumstances. Since the completion of the Seal Beach project plans, the State Coastal Conservancy has initiated several more community participation projects. In the City of Oceanside, citizens planned the restoration of the mile-long Strand beachfront, a project which included a citizen-judged competition to choose an architect for the project. In the City of Coronado, citizens completed a plan for a 16-acre area adjoining Glorietta Bay.[2] In the San Francisco Bay area, participants from four cities agreed on one integrated plan for the East Bay shoreline. Yet another project is under way in the City of Santa Monica. With these projects, the Coastal Conservancy has developed a successful method for involving citizens in redesigning urban waterfronts on the coast of California.

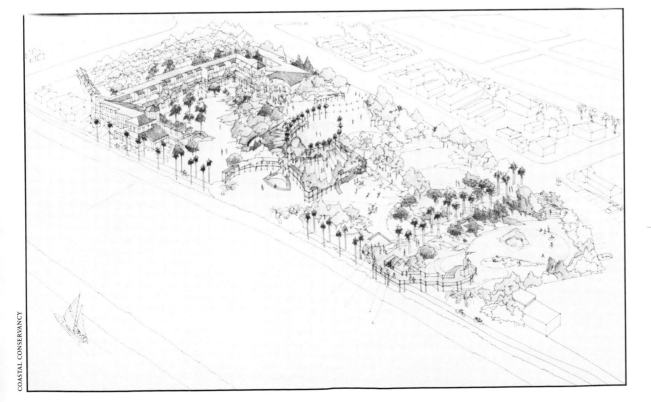

COASTAL CONSERVANCY

In a seminal article on community living called "The Politics of Place," Karl Hess revives René Dubos' injunction "think globally, act locally."[3] Hess argues eloquently that local political and economic action is the most effective arena for change. What is evolving is an effective and pragmatic process of involving communities in environmental change. To date, the community participation model has had its most successful applications in southern California, an area where citizen apathy toward environmental quality was thought to have reached its zenith. The community participation process is clearly applicable to coastal environments, including waterfronts. In California and throughout the country, coastal resources are receiving greater protection as the demands for public access and use, and thus public input, become more and more emphatic.

But community participation has its limits. It does not work well in instances where public policy aims to relocate residents and businesses. As a planning process it is much better at renewal than removal. It is probably not a useful approach for a project with an immediate negative impact on the environment, though it has been used for power plant siting. Neither is it very effective in long-range, general plans where the environmental impacts and benefits are too remote or vague.

Community participation is not yet a common practice. In 1976, Arrowstreet, an architecture/planning firm, undertook a national study with Environmental Design Group. In it they asked the question, "Is there a participatory design movement?" The answer, after a year's review of the state of the art, was that some established firms are actively doing participatory work, but "the vast majority of architectural firms have not for whatever reasons taken steps to increase user input in their work."[4]

Recent reviews in the *American Institute of Planners Journal* of four current books on citizen participation conclude that no work on the subject "integrates both theory and practice in a positive and holistic manner useful to both academics and practitioners."[5]

New models for participation are clearly needed. A practice should be established that suits the ideals of participation and gets the desired results: producing better designs and more efficient and equitable implementation. It is time for participation to be recognized as a tool for positive change and enhancement of community. As the California Legislature declared in the Coastal Act of 1976:

> "The Legislature further finds and declares that the public has a right to fully participate in decisions affecting coastal planning, conservation, and develop-

ment; that achievement of sound coastal conservation and development is dependent upon public understanding and support; and that the continuing planning and implementation of programs for coastal conservation and development should include the widest opportunity for public participation."[6]

Principles of Community Participation

Community participation can be defined as "the practice of involving as many people as possible through consensus-building workshops in the planning, design, and implementation of environmental change to a specific area in a community." In Conservancy community participation projects, we have found the following six elements, which offer parameters for those who want to define a community participation project and determine a method to accomplish it.

Locality: Locality has two aspects: the project area or site and the community of people who identify with that place. To be successful, the project should focus on a specific area and involve the local community. The area typically would be under-utilized, deteriorating, or environmentally threatened from a public and/or private standpoint. While the Conservancy was constrained by law to deal with policies and land use issues that had statewide as well as local importance, participants were drawn almost exclusively from city residents and primarily from coastal neighborhoods. Community participants tend to think less defensively and more in terms of their community, as they define it. This definition of community often extends beyond the local political boundary and takes into account visitors attracted to the area.

Maximum Participation: A basic, and perhaps obvious principle of community participation is the encouragement of maximum participation. Publicity of workshops must be as wide and thorough as possible. The greater the number and the broader the representation of the participants, the more defensible the ultimate plan.

The workshop format and the immediacy of the project tend to attract more attendance than most community meetings. The community participation workshop structure can adjust to serve the size of the group, which in the Conservancy's experience has varied from 60 to 200 people. Rather than limit participation by selecting special interest group representatives or meeting with organized groups individually, the community participation process assumes everyone can work together and requires that everyone work together in one room.

Healthy paranoia and self-interest contribute to the community's interest in the participation process, and the process can harness those feelings. The threat of unwanted change remains a universal organizing principle. Non-participation is an equally important part of this principle. Citizens who don't attend the workshops are in a weak position, and they know it. If they don't participate, they can't complain later.

Expertise: In community participation, the experts are community members; professionals from the outside act as agents of change. Respect for the expert knowledge of the local participants is essential. They are closest to the situation; they are usually the most frequent users of the project area and they will become primarily responsible for implementation under the community participation process.

The community is the professionals' client during the workshops, and the professionals' expertise is used to show whether the workshop participants' ideas can be visualized and realized. A typical community participation consultant team would include an architect or landscape architect, a planner, an economist, and a public involvement specialist. Probably most difficult is the role of the community participation organizer, often a planner or architect who must develop

new professional skills for such a situation. Workshop organizers soon realize that conducting, scoring, facilitating, and leading workshops are demanding tasks requiring special ability and professionalism.

Design: In the community workshop, participants actually draw and construct their ideas. Design consultants synthesize, sketch, or model alternatives and ultimately respond to the consensus with a conceptual plan of what the project could look like. Participation is greatly enhanced by going beyond planning concepts and written proposals to graphic visualization and hands-on involvement. Design is an essential link in the workshop between the participants' verbal ideas and implementation mechanisms. Designs clarify goals for the participants without necessarily tying decision makers to the details. The completion of a design is essential to help the planner and designer understand what the community wants.

Economics: Economic considerations become a decision-making tool in the community participation process. Participants must be made aware of the costs and potential financing of their recommendations. Economic games, charts, and

The citizens were encouraged to build their own rough models of design ideas, such as the one shown at right. The cartoon below, showing a "superman" state agency flying to the rescue of local citizens, was drawn at the beginning of the workshop conference, before the citizens came to realize that state assistance could only help them to assume responsibility for their community themselves.

COASTAL CONSERVANCY

COASTAL CONSERVANCY

matrices were invented for each Conservancy project to clarify a variety of choices such as: minimum versus maximum development; now versus later projects; in-hand funds versus uncertain grants; private taxes, leases, and/or revenue bonds; federal, state, and/or local grants and their priorities; and land use and design choices that affect the market or competitiveness for grants. Developers, bankers, and administrators of government grant programs should be included as resources in the workshops to elucidate alternatives and risks before decisions are made.

The economic "reality test," as Conservancy Executive Officer Joseph Petrillo calls it, has led to many creative solutions and more responsible recommendations. Fear of delays by community opponents can be, of course, a primary motive for developers to cooperate in community participation projects. And successful developers, whether large or small, are of necessity becoming more receptive to the community. If community participation allows for more predictable timing and a reasonable outcome, then it will be embraced for economic reasons.

Developers, government officials, and architects should be aware of more positive reasons to support community participation. Participants in a community workshop process have a positive and active rather than reactive role in arriving at development decisions. Responsibility, an important theme of community participation, is encouraged in two ways. First, the process enables the participant to balance the potential of public grants and the fiscal health of the city against the ability of private development to contribute directly or indirectly to the public benefits desired. Secondly, participants not only make recommendations on the allocation of public and private funds, they participate in the implementation of their recommendations. In the Conservancy's projects, citizen task forces of workshop participants have played a strong role in implementation. The education they receive in the workshop process enabled them to speed up the approval process, lobby effectively, justify grants, and make necessary adjustments with developers, all benefits to hard-pressed city staffs.

Structure: A basic strength of community participation, in contrast to many other participation techniques, is that it is structured to arrive at a decision that can be implemented. Community participants must arrive at their own recommendations, given an awareness of regulatory, time, and money constraints. This is a basic concomitant of the workshops. The general structure includes a team of consultants, publicity, a bank of consensus building tools and facts for the participants to use, and finally a product in the form of a project design and financing package. Three to five monthly workshops are usually sufficient. Within this general structure, each project is designed to fit unique circumstances. Within each project, a wide variety of techniques is used to avoid manipulating the conclusions of the workshop. Any heavy-handed closure of discussion or inability to be patient with this initially more time-consuming but open process will reduce the quality and quantity of participation. The facilitator must recognize disagreement and conflict in the quest for common approaches. Participation is intrinsically expansive—the more inclusive it is the more effective it is. The forging of agreement is understandably contagious and it builds confidence in the ability to implement proposals.

Space does not permit a full description of the numerous techniques that give structure to each workshop, insure the creative participation of each individual, and reveal areas of agreement between participants. Awareness walks, transference of work and responsibility to the participants, recognition of conflict and antagonism, fantasy scores, reality scores, role-playing, group graphics, feedback, recognition, active listening, facilitation, agreement versus voting, and the use of play and celebration—these are just a few of the techniques of consensus building, many of which were first integrated by the Take Part Process.

A Pragmatic Approach

A community participation project has a certain underlying integrity: (1) it is achievable within a limited time and place; (2) real decisions are made in the process, giving credibility

Seal Beach citizens visit the site of their workshop-planned development.

JUDY GRAEME

HELP PLAN WHERE THE RIVER MEETS THE SEA

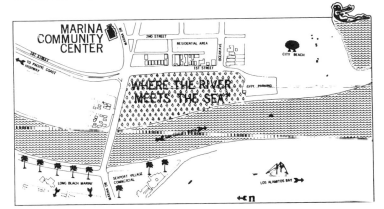

JOIN A SERIES OF COMMUNITY PLANNING WORKSHOPS TO PLAN AND DESIGN WHAT SHOULD HAPPEN ON THE OLD D.W.P. SITE ! ! ! ! !

SPONSORED BY THE STATE COASTAL CONSERVANCY

AT THE INVITATION OF THE CITY OF SEAL BEACH, THE SAN GABRIEL-PACIFIC PARKS SOCIETY, AND OTHERS.

FIRST WORKSHOPS : FRIDAY, DECEMBER 1, 1978 7:30 - 10:00 PM   AND
SATURDAY, DECEMBER 2,1978 9:30 AM - 4:30 PM

WORKSHOPS WILL CONTINUE IN JANUARY, FEBRUARY, AND MARCH ! ! !

LOCATION : MARINA COMMUNITY CENTER, MARINA DRIVE, SEAL BEACH

DESIGN AND PLANNING TEAM: MOORE RUBLE YUDELL, ARCHITECTS & PLANNERS   WORKSHOPS COORDINATOR : JIM BURNS

COME HELP PLAN A MAJOR PART OF YOUR FUTURE ENVIRONMENT IN SEAL BEACH !

SEAL BEACH

COASTAL CONSERVANCY

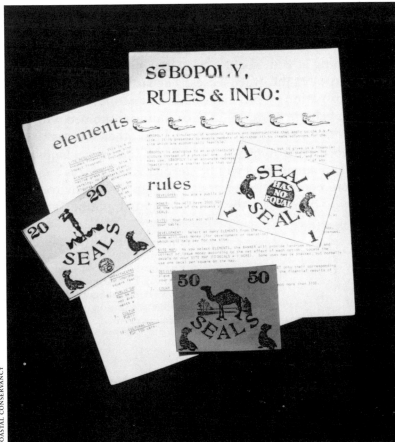

COASTAL CONSERVANCY

and power to those who participate; and (3) it parallels political and economic forces moving toward local responsibility. Community participation has a pragmatic appeal. That appeal extends to government, which must be more efficient in the use of staff and financial resources. More than anything else, it is a process for the community that wants or needs to collaborate successfully with government and business. It is a process for people who want to expand their understanding of, and ability to improve their community. Lastly, it is a process by which government can better encourage constructive citizen action in solving coastal problems, while making more efficient and productive use of scarce public resources. Community participation has worked in fostering innovative and improved design of the coastal environment. ●

Notes:

1. Lawrence Halprin and Jim Burns, *Take Part: A Workshop Approach to Collective Creativity* (The MIT Press, 1974).

2. Gayle Kidder, "Coronado: the Rainmaker, the Sheriff's Posse, and the Wizard of Oz," *San Diego Magazine,* 34(2), p. 151.

3. Karl Hess, "Politics of Place," *Coevolution Quarterly,* Summer 1981, pp. 4–16.

4. Arrowstreet, "Another Side of Architecture," *Progressive Architecture,* December 1976, p. 68

5. Ann DeWitt Watts and Ellen W. Steiss, Review of: Michael Fagence, *Citizen Participation in Planning* (Oxford: Pergamon Press, 1977); J. M. Simmie, *Citizens in Conflict: The Sociology of Town Planning* (New York: Hutchinson and Company, 1974); Joseph Lee Rogers, Jr., *Citizen Committees: A Guide to their Use in Local Government* (Cambridge, MA: Ballinger, 1977); and W. R. Derrick Sewell and J. T. Coppock, *Public Participation in Planning* (New York: John Wiley and Sons, 1977) in the *American Institute of Planners Journal,* October 1978.

6. California Coastal Act of 1976, Public Resources Code Section 30006, Division 20.

that are inappropriate to the lives and uses of the people who will visit or inhabit them. This chapter, then, is to help you who live in coastal communities to become aware of the most appropriate ways of conserving, preserving, and changing your environments. Awareness is your beginning.

Some of the communities in this essay have dealt imaginatively with the problems and potentials of their seaside environments; some are communities which have yet to approach them in positive ways. You will find much here about improved access and connections between people and their natural environments. While I fully agree with the need for undisturbed natural coastal preserves, my interest here is in making many seaside environments part of living communities, not isolated places which people can view but not touch. This chapter explores the human use and enjoyment of more urban seaside environments.

The communities in this essay fall within three basic situations:

- relationships of community, seashore, and land configurations;
- community connections with natural and historic resources; and
- the impact of man-made change on coastal communities.

Relationships of Community, Seashore, and Land Configurations

Capitola (Santa Cruz County) sits on slopes around its little cove like the Cornwall cove-towns of St. Ives and Polperro. Like them, Capitola is the right scale relationship to its natural configuration of cliffs, cove, beach, river, and bay. Structures around Capitola's cove are appropriately densely-sited and village-like, following the generally circular forms of the topography. An old railroad bridge and a vehicular bridge form strong structural backdrops for the view from the cove. The Soquel River empties into Monterey Bay here and is wisely treated as a special event in the landscape-seascape.

The fields around Capitola are noted for the production of begonias, and there is an annual Begonia Festival at the blossoms' height. The highlight of the Festival is a parade of begonia-bedecked floats down the river to the cove.

Capitola's respect for its special environment has resulted in a community with its focus where it should be: on its beach and cove. Its use of the begonia harvest, another natural resource, provides a reason to celebrate in this very special environment. Capitola takes advantage of its special site.

Not all coastal communities have the natural advantages of Capitola. Communities with flat terrain have problems with identity and visibility. They seem two-dimensional. Anything that introduces three-dimensionality becomes the image or symbol of the place. For example, the highly visible and dramatic grain silos in towns on the Great Plains establish an identity for these locations. In communities like Imperial Beach (San Diego County), where visitors are seeking a goal (i.e., the beach), this two-dimensionality can cause a vague sense of disorientation or unease. There is no image that says, "Here comes the beach," and no environmental transition to make the approach to the beach one of pleasure and heightening expectation.

Imperial Beach is a low-slung town of one and two-story structures, many of them sparsely spaced in the beach area. Generally flat urban terrain leads to a generally flat beach. Access is simple, but there is little character, texture, or interest to the community and its beach environment. But even in a case like Imperial Beach, there is no reason to introduce an imported symbol or an extravagant Disneyesque environment to provide the attraction to lead people to the water's edge. Natural materials and appropriately-scaled beach facilities can provide this and upgrade the rest of the community environment as well.

In Imperial Beach and other coastal communities, gateways, entries, and passageways to the seaside can utilize tall palms, landscaping, arcades, and trellises to achieve significant results with modest means. There is another message here. Access to the seashore's resources is important, but the quality of that access is equally important. It should be pleasurable, elegant, fun, thrilling, or whatever is the appropriate quality of the particular community and its environment.

Pismo Beach boasts many recreational and environmental opportunities, but the way the town meets the beach leaves much to be desired.

JIM BURNS

Many other California beaches are perceived *and* approached via sloping or terraced configurations of the topography. In these towns, visitors can see the shore from a distance, but access can still be a problem.

In Pismo Beach (San Luis Obispo County), motorists on Highway 101 become aware of the town and the beach downslope below them as they drive north or south. Access to the town from the freeway is uncomplicated, but getting through downtown Pismo Beach to reach the shore can be a little confusing. To assist bewildered visitors, Pismo Beach can better direct people to its various recreational treasures. Visual announcements of the specific delights available down the slope should be provided along Highway 101. For people who enjoy the visitor-serving commercial attractions of a resort community, improved and more specific visual information and an upgraded connection of Pomeroy Street (the main east-west street) would emphasize the resort nature of Pismo Beach. The public pier at the bottom of Pomeroy Street would be greatly enhanced with a small green public park at the pier head (presently unused derelict space).

Community Connections with Natural and Historic Resources

Gualala, just north of the Sonoma-Mendocino county line, is blessed with a wealth of scenic and natural resources. The town is atop medium-height bluffs along the ocean on historic Highway 1. From the densely wooded hills at its back flows the Gualala River. Between the river and the ocean, stretching almost the length of the community, is a spectacular sand spit populated by hundreds of sea birds and coruscated by fantastic forms of driftwood and timber washed up by the wild surf. It provides a feast for the senses. The peninsula is connected to the mainland at its south end, where ocean meadows and forests join it to form Gualala Point County Park. Gualala itself is a charmingly unimproved community whose chief man-made adornment is the old Gualala Hotel, which faces the bluffs, river, sand spit, and ocean from the center of town.

Gualala is an example of a town that lacks adequate access to the abundant resources around it. The town's man-made delights connect only visually with its natural resources. A stronger physical connection would make a stop in Gualala a highlight of a trip up the North Coast.

About an acre of vacant land atop the bluff directly across the Gualala Hotel would make an ideal public overlook-park. A series of easily negotiated zig-zag ramps descending from the park would provide access to the river's edge. From there, people could reach the spit via a pontoon bridge (rising and falling with the changing volumes of water in the river) or a

pedestrian ferry operated on cables attached to each shore. Thus, people could have more than one choice of how to enjoy the special confluence of natural resources Gualala offers.

The need to provide good connections between the community and its natural and man-made recreational resources is certainly not limited to Gualala. Point Arena (Mendocino County) is a small coastal community that has retained much of the feel it must have had 50 years ago as a timber and fishing town. In addition to its tiny downtown, Point Arena also has two special resources that could be upgraded or made more available: Arena Cove and the Point Arena Lighthouse. Arena Cove, Point Arena's minuscule fishing port and pier area, is one mile down Port Road from Main Street (Highway 1). The cove has a pier, a cafe, some rental units, warehouses or old canneries, a few houses, and—a bit inland along Port Road—mobile homes evidently used by fishermen and their families. The beach is rough shingle; the pier and most of the buildings are in bad shape; the mobile homes are inappropriately located and in danger from flooding. Despite these problems, this cove has drama and interest; it affects all the senses strongly. The community of Point Arena would benefit if the cove were made more accessible, if some of the facilities (especially the pier, cafe, and transient units) were improved, and if the mobile homes were relocated elsewhere. The delicate problem is: How can this be done without destroying the rough-and-ready charm of the place and without making it such a tourist lure that its singular qualities are wiped out? The one-mile stretch between downtown and Arena Cove is in almost totally natural condition—a delightful canyon with a stream along its bottom. The City should prohibit all building and any other uses (such as the mobile homes) which detract from this area's natural qualities. Care must be taken to eliminate or control the flooding hazard, water quality, and other concerns which exist in this tight-knit environment. Thus, the connection to a somewhat upgraded Arena Cove would remain a "wild" natural environment. This would reduce future building impacts on the canyon and cove alike.

The Point Arena Lighthouse is several miles north, off the Coast Road. The lighthouse is reached via a spectacularly scenic ride or hike through farmlands to a dramatic peninsula. Unfortunately, the lighthouse itself, under U.S. Coast Guard jurisdiction, is off limits to the public. This is a disappointment to people who make the two-mile trek out to visit the structure. With cooperation between the community, the State, and the Coast Guard, people would be free to visit a splendid and historic structure and picnic on the grounds at its base.

The Urban Edge

The Impact of Man-made Change on Coastal Communities

Santa Barbara (Santa Barbara County) has just accomplished an admirable resuscitation of its storm-damaged old Stearns Wharf. But a problem common to many seaside communities still plagues Santa Barbara: how to improve access to the beach area from downtown across man-made barriers such as highways and railroad tracks. Though these barriers do not prevent access, they make the journey to the beach less pleasant. Unfortunately, many of the usual solutions come with problems attached. A pedestrian-vehicular tunnel passing under Highway 101 and the tracks would be costly, and more problematic, may have structural problems in a location with a high water table.

A pedestrian-vehicular bridge making the same connection would also be costly. A bridge would have to be inordinately high to permit passage of tall vehicles, but this would block the marine view from downtown. A vehicular bypass or alternate routing for large vehicles might make the bridge overpass option more feasible, but possible routes are quite extensively developed.

Another possible solution would be to keep all vehicles on grade and let them continue to fight the stoplight and intersection battle, but make provisions for pedestrians and lighter, smaller vehicles (e.g., bikes, people movers) wishing to gain beach access. Pedestrian-bike-small vehicle overpass bridges at State Street and other main connections to the beach area would be less expensive than massive vehicular overpasses. They could also be more airy, "transparent" designs which block less of the views. Given expert designers, they might even become "entrance" symbols for Santa Barbara to travelers on Highway 101.

A more subtle "interruption" between Santa Barbara and its beach and Stearns Wharf is the almost exclusive use of the area between 101 and the beach for motels and a few restaurants. Downtown Santa Barbara is justly noted as one of the most charming and lively communities on the California coast. But the area between the highway and the water does not share this vivacity. We saw earlier that the quality of access is important—but this part of town, a kind of transient "ghetto," detracts from the quality of access. A more varied mix of uses in this area would be valued by day visitors and by residents. A change in the use complexion here would bring some of the liveliness on the town side of State Street down to the water's edge.

Man-made interventions in the landscape—even when they do not block access to the water—can affect the quality of life in a coastal community. On the approach to the tiny community of Moss Landing (Monterey County), a gigantic form

juts out of the landscape, as though a gargantuan supernatural chessplayer left one of his castles behind to weather on a seaside chess board. This is a huge power plant of the Pacific Gas & Electric Company. Reaching Moss Landing, the disparity in scale is even more astonishing. On one side of Highway 1, the power plant rears into the sky, emitting towering plumes of steam. On the other side, clustered around Moss Landing's inlet, is a bustling fishing and canning industry, a busy marina, a few tourist-oriented businesses. This immense PG&E presence and its traditional fishing-recreational neighbor make a very odd couple. But strangely, it seems to work. PG&E and the fishing village keep to their own sides of the highway. The power plant is held back from the water, leaving the shoreline and inlet as a water-oriented commercial and recreational resource.

In other cases, the larger and more powerful of such a combination may present a danger to the community. The power plant in Morro Bay is not so amenable a presence as that in Moss Landing; it looms too uncomfortably and obtrusively in its community. Here, as well as in Carlsbad and El Segundo, the massive presence intrudes too close to the water. There is not the cordial and appropriate separation of scale that exists in Moss Landing. In Fort Bragg, the Georgia Pacific timber operation consumes almost the entire waterfront, cutting the downtown off from access to the seashore. Though this is presently a problem, it can prove a future benefit. When Georgia Pacific exhausts its need to be in Fort Bragg, the community should take care that the land it occupies is turned to the public weal. In Huntington Beach and to the north, oil pumping machinery on the beaches and oil rigs in the sea are hideous physical intrusions as well as potential polluters. Their presence could be alleviated visually somewhat by painting and caricaturing them in the way the rigs off Long Beach have been.

A far more problematic intrusion of giant man-made objects into or near seaside communities is presented by nuclear power plants. The Diablo Canyon plant in San Luis Obispo County has gained widespread and deserved notoriety for slipshod planning of a dangerous facility whose need has never been fully established. Its gigantic mass hulking on the water's edge is a visual symbol of its deadly potential. In addition to its more important lethal aspects, the visual impact of such a place has been little considered. More intensive and dispassionate investigation into the consequences of such gigantic seaside objects must govern their future creation more than in the careless past.

Our final example, Monterey (Monterey County), has just about all the components any resort community could wish

Pismo Dunes at the waterline

Gualala, California

Smugglers Cove

Clamming Capital

Pismo Beach

Taking a Closer Look at Your Town

In his description of coastal towns, Jim Burns discusses several important considerations for coastal communities. The following questions may help you apply these considerations to your own community.

Access:

Does your town provide easy approaches to the shore for pedestrians and vehicles?

Do barriers—man-made or natural—block the way to the water?

Are the routes to the shore clearly marked?

Do traffic and parking pose problems near the waterfront?

Are appropriate access facilities provided? (These include stairs or ramps to the beach, trails, picnic facilities, fishing, boating, viewing, restrooms, etc.)

Are parts of your town linked by easy-to-follow routes?

Identity:

Does your town have a visual identity? Does it look like a coastal town? What *kind* of coastal town?

Does the approach to the shore provide a sense of transition, identifying this as the way to the waterfront?

Are the scales of your town and its environment compatible?

Does your town make use of festivals, celebrations, and other special events to provide a sense of community identity?

Resources:

Are your town's natural resources accessible to the public?

Have steps been taken to protect or restore cultural and historical resources and open space?

Have facilities been provided to allow visitors to make use of the town's recreational potential?

Community Involvement:

Are citizens involved in planning the future of their own community?

The Urban Edge

for: an historic district restored to much of its original character; a thriving central business district; a fisherman's wharf area; downtown parks and beaches; fishing piers and facilities; hotels, motels, theaters, and a new convention center; and historic Cannery Row, soon to boast a new aquarium.

Sad to say, Monterey is one of the most aggravating towns on the California coast to get around in and appreciate all of these splendid opportunities. Congested streets, twisted roadways, confusing ramps on and off highways slashing through the community, a tunnel that sweeps the unwary past several of the main locations, and major local attractions unconnected by any sort of accessible movement pattern—all these contribute to a sense of frustration and anger for the visitor. The local taxi industry must thrive on the helplessness of those unfamiliar with how to get around in Monterey.

One simple partial solution could be instituted without much bother or expense. A pedestrian and bicycle way could run along the city's main shoreline from the new aquarium at the western end of Cannery Row all the way past the fishing pier and Fisherman's Wharf to Monterey State Beach and El Estero Park at the eastern end of downtown. Since there is a good, walkable connection from Fisherman's Wharf to the old historic district, downtown, and the hotel-convention areas, this modest biking-walking path along the shore of the bay would perform the miracle of connecting the pieces of Monterey's recreational and historical resources. Happily, a project to make these connections is currently under way. Monterey, Pacific Grove, and the Monterey Regional Parks District have contacted the Coastal Conservancy about the possibility of shoreline walkways and bike paths; use of the existing railroad tracks at the water's edge for a trolley all the way to Asilomar State Beach along the old Southern Pacific right-of-way has also been proposed.

Take Action: Examine Your Community

You who live in seaside communities have a very particular responsibility, not only to yourselves but to all of us, to care for these special environments. Your care and creativity in examining and planning for your own community's seaside can help guarantee its magical qualities for succeeding generations. What ultimately counts are your answers to six questions.

- Have I made myself aware, through all my senses, of what is happening to the coastal environment of my community?

- Do I perceive needs and possibilities in the coastal environment of my community?

- Do I care about doing something about improving the place where I live?

- Will I make contacts and involve others in these important activities?

- Am I going to get moving now and take responsibility for seeing that what should happen, actually happens?

- If you have answered yes to all or some of the above, will you look into how natural and man-made resources relate, how design and planning can improve your seashore, and start to develop a process whereby your community can give its best to caring for your unique environment?

I hope that you got six positive answers. If so, you are on your way. Good luck! ●

At Moss Landing, the PG&E power plant, as shown above, looms over the fishing fleet in its cove. Beach access over the dunes at Moss Landing is achieved by the delightful series of simple wooden platforms seen at right.

The Urban Edge

Elements of Capitola to Compare to Your Community:

Advantages & Potentials

Good scale relationships.

Good river-bay connection.

Use of environment for festivals and celebrations.

Tight density of buildings around cove.

Town terraces back from cove.

Small streets slow and control traffic.

Problems

Heavy traffic in season.

Lack of sympathetic connections with parts of town outside cove area.

Elements of Santa Barbara to Compare to Your Community:

Advantages & Potentials

The town has a superb beachfront and imaginatively reconstructed Stearns Wharf.

Downtown Santa Barbara is a lively and inviting environment with adequate tourist provisions.

Problems

Beach and wharf are separated from most of community by heavily used highway and railroad.

Area between highway and beach offers few uses for townspeople or day

Elements of Gualala to Compare to Your Community:

Advantages & Potentials

Community and resources are not over-developed or "improved."

Potentially usable public open space exists in center of town.

Options for access to spit can be increased.

Historic hotel is still in use and good condition.

Problems

More options for enjoyment of community and resources needed.

Town center currently lacks public open space.

Town currently lacks direct access to sand spit across river.

Connection between hotel, potential public park, and access to sand spit needed.

Elements of Moss Landing to Compare to Your Community:

Advantages & Potentials

Moss Landing has a thriving fishing and marina activity.

PG&E power plant is a sort of crazy "sculpture" in low-scale landscape.

Gigantic seaside objects can be interesting diversions, as in case of Moss Landing, or present possibility of repeating Mendocino model, as at Fort Bragg.

Problems

The town could be overwhelmed by neighboring PG&E power plant.

Any future growth or expansion of plant should be carefully studied and inhibited.

Gigantic seaside objects can be intrusions and even potentially lethal. Smaller intrusions can be just as deadly or visually offensive, like a leaky sewage plant or an inappropriately sited and maintained polluting industry.

Elements of Monterey to Compare to Your Community:

Advantages & Potentials

Many prime recreational and cultural opportunities for visitors and residents.

Shoreline of Monterey Bay is an ideal site for a pedestrian-bike trail to connect waterside sites.

Cannery Row is a major resource for tourism and community. New aquarium will contribute greatly.

Problems

Recreational opportunities are separated by dismaying and frustrating network of vehicular ways.

Such a trail does not exist.

Cannery Row's potentials are underutilized because of difficulty of access. Some potentials such as old hotel are also unrealized.

Notes:

1. Oliver Goldsmith, "The Traveller," line 282.

Section Three
Financing Waterfront Restoration

"Amenities are **the** *economics of the city."*
— James Rouse

The previous essays described successful public efforts to stimulate design compatible with coastal conditions and values, as articulated in the California Coastal Act. Urban waterfronts have received a major share of this recent attention because of their historic and economic importance, their great resource value, and their importance as growing population centers. Local governments and private investors are rediscovering waterfronts as potentially valuable resources. A significant aspect of this rediscovery is that waterfront design—and designs for the waterfront—are beginning to reflect the natural advantages of the waterfront location.

The following essays point out that the revitalization of a waterfront is linked to the city's economic health, and show how a city can afford waterfront redevelopment even in an age of austerity. Robert McNulty and Patricia Hunter describe how amenities—that is, tangible public benefits in the form of facilities, settings, and activities—benefit not only city residents, but also the city's economic health. Amenities are now being used by public agencies as economic development tools, along with financial packaging, tax incentives, site acquisition and development, and other conventional approaches. Peter Epstein describes in detail a variety of possible methods and techniques for providing amenities as an integral part of waterfront development. Clearly, the public sector has a crucial role to play in achieving compatible waterfront designs and, indeed, all coastal design. That role involves entrepreneurial and mediating behavior that is not typical of government, but which government is nonetheless capable of learning. It includes preparing the ground— literally, as well as politically and financially—for the development to come. Of necessity, government is taking the overall management role in waterfront design and development.

Compatible waterfront design that includes public amenities, far from being a costly luxury, is now being considered by both the public and private sector as an essential—and leading—part of waterfront development.

The Value of Amenities: Waterfront Restoration Can Pay Off

Robert H. McNulty
and Patricia A. Hunter

The phoenix-like revival of urban waterfronts makes them one of the most attractive opportunities for public and private investment today. The comeback is an interesting one because it is based, in most cases, on a perception of the waterfront as an amenity, both for the citizen and for the developer.

To the citizen, amenities are tangible assets that enrich lives and make a place more pleasant. Cultural and recreational opportunities, such as festivals, boating, and fishing, are amenities; as are facilities, such as maritime museums, aquariums, marinas, and historic ships; and as are settings, such as parks, plazas, and promenades. These amenities are usually provided by government for the public good.

To a developer, "amenity" has a slightly different meaning. It is a characteristic of a particular site that makes that site more valuable than another. A waterfront site has a built-in amenity in its location, and developers are discovering that they can multiply the value of that basic amenity by providing others for the public.

On the waterfront, amenities have become an economic development tool for local officials. Amenities attract private development, giving cities the means to attract new business, jobs, and tax revenue, even as they enhance recreational use of water and shoreline. Without amenities, waterfront commerce attracts fewer people, workers are less productive, business flees to the suburbs, jobs disappear, and revenues plummet.

Amenities are not the only economic tool for waterfront revitalization. There are other weapons in a city's economic development arsenal—tax incentives, guaranteed loans, financial packaging, land acquisition, site development, street and sewer construction, among others. The value of urban amenities as economic tools has been growing in the public awareness for several decades, and has come to be accepted by most local planners.

An unprecedented 1979 research study on the urban impact of federal policies conducted by the Rand Corporation made the case convincingly that jobs—and therefore economic health—tend to follow people to the places where the quality of life is high.[1] Before the Rand study, cities generally had based local economic development strategies on attracting industry. Today, more and more cities are concentrating on building local amenities and local city image.

Recent efforts have concerned almost all facets of the quality of life—from cultural facilities, to restored historic buildings, to parks and open space.[2] In Oakland, California, for example, city leaders are creating a linear sculpture park as an economic development tool. Paterson, New Jersey has restored and redeveloped its historic industrial buildings to attract tourists. St. Louis, Missouri is redeveloping its declining midtown area to become a regional cultural district, and Indianapolis is using the White River Park as the focus for regional economic development efforts.

Because much of the waterfront's value to a developer lies in the location's value as an amenity, developing the other amenities of the area is often the best way to attract and support quality waterfront development. Here, perhaps more than anywhere else in the city, amenities have a profound influence on business success, worker productivity, and a host of other economic factors. Developer James Rouse is direct about the economic importance of amenities. "The amenities," he says, "are *the* economics of the city."

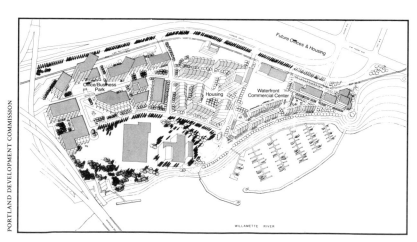

PORTLAND DEVELOPMENT COMMISSION

Portland's urban waterfront plan emphasizes a return to the water after years of deterioration. The plan replaces an expressway with a series of public amenities focused on a waterfront park. Government strategy is to develop the public amenities first, thereby stimulating private investment in commercial and residential development. What had become an unused waterfront will soon become a center of urban and restaurant facilities, homes, a marina, and open space and public access.

At middle right is an 1827 lithograph of the east view of Faneuil Hall in Boston. Below left and at bottom are views of the site after extensive restoration efforts by The Rouse Company to create another "festive marketplace." In contrast to Baltimore's Harborplace, which largely consists of entirely new development, Boston's Faneuil Hall project focused on restoring the historic structures of the original waterfront and adapting them for modern commercial use and public enjoyment.

An aerial view of the site of Harborplace in Baltimore (right), developed by The Rouse Company in cooperation with the City. The City began early to provide the foundation for this "festive marketplace" on the waterfront by developing a series of public amenities which subsequently attracted the attention of private developers to the potential of the site.

The Festive Marketplace

Rouse should know. Of all the new types of development to hit the waterfront, none has created more excitement and profit than the Rouse Company's Harborplace in Baltimore and Faneuil Hall Marketplace in Boston. These and other "festive marketplaces" combine commerce and amenities with great showmanship. Since many older city markets were once located near the waterfront, to be near the source of goods and produce, the marketplace theme and amenities that complement it make good sense.

This proximity of waterfront and marketplace has made Harborplace a success, but long before Rouse spotted the potential of the Inner Harbor, the city began laying the groundwork by developing the harbor area's amenities. Nine years ago, Baltimore's Inner Harbor was an abandoned wasteland. No developers were interested in it. The city, however, was anxious to expand its downtown revitalization to the nearby waterfront, and planned for the Inner Harbor a variety of public events. Festivals, concerts, boat races, and public facilities like a promenade, playing fields, marina, historic ships, etc. were planned to encourage entrepreneurial interest in the area. Events such as the Baltimore City Fair and the city's many ethnic festivals began to attract people to the Inner Harbor in droves, and developers began to be interested in the possible profit from these visitors.

The Rouse Company turned these possible profits into reality with Harborplace, a commercial and retail "festival marketplace" consisting of two pavilions with 12 restaurants and 45 shops on the corner of the Inner Harbor nearest the downtown. The sales per square foot are the highest of any of the Rouse Company's retail centers. The development created 2,331 jobs, and more than 800 of them were filled by the city's jobless. During the first year the project generated $3 million in state sales tax and $1.5 million in city property taxes.

Other effects of the city's commitment to amenities in the Inner Harbor have been tremendous. A study completed in 1980 by the Real Estate Research Corporation, showed that two out of three people coming for the fairs and festivals were from outside the city—and those people spent $125 million while enjoying the city. Baltimore is now a major tourist attraction, thanks to the Inner Harbor developments and the new perception of Baltimore as a "festival city."

A Hyatt Hotel recently opened near the Inner Harbor. The hotel worked closely with the city's Office of Manpower to hire minority and jobless individuals. So powerful is the draw of the Inner Harbor that the hotel is already 120 percent booked. The National Aquarium, opened in 1981, exceeded first-year revenue projections in the first four months.

Baltimore paid for its public amenities out of public funds. The promenade, marina, and finger piers were constructed with state and local funds and urban renewal block grant money. The aquarium was built with money from the U.S. Department of Commerce and a city bond issue. The initial development of the Baltimore City Fair was funded by the National Endowment for the Arts. The city donates police and sanitation services for festivals, and other festival operating funds come from private-sector donations and booth rentals. Maintenance of public spaces and amenities is the responsibility of the Department of Recreation and Parks, although the Rouse Company maintains its own pavilion areas.

Baltimore's Inner Harbor development works because its amenities are what people wanted. They meet economic and social needs of the community, suit the natural resources of the water and shore, and they take advantage of the city's unique historic features. A similar solution is under way in New York City's South Street Seaport area. The eleven-block area of eighteenth and nineteenth century buildings includes several piers, a fleet of historic ships, and the Fulton Fish Market. The development is sponsored by the South Street Seaport Museum.

With the revival of the South Street Seaport, people who never thought it safe or possible to come to this waterfront are being drawn by the fleet of historic ships, the educational programs about the Great Age of Sail of the 1850s, and the special events on the piers. These special events, which receive private support, include evening jazz concerts that attract visitors to an area that was previously considered a place to be avoided after dark.

The revival of the seaport area brought the Rouse Company again into the picture. The Rouse development will feature shops in a new marketplace pavilion on the piers and in restored buildings. Planners estimate that the development will cost from $250 to $270 million, and enormous profits are expected. The City of New York hopes for $10 million in taxes, while New York State expects $6.5 million in taxes on the Rouse Company's $150 million in annual sales. By the time the project is completed, planners expect it to create more than 1,700 construction jobs and some 4,000 permanent jobs. The South Street Seaport Museum, which has control over development quality and types of merchandise to be sold in shops, will get ten percent of the gross rents immediately, and later a share of the net income.

Two other important aspects of the South Street Seaport project are the retention of the Fulton Fish Market and the provision of sea-level dining in the Rouse development.

Rouse's vice president for public affairs, Scott Ditch, points out that in a city with thousands of restaurants, more are hardly an amenity; a new restaurant would not make this site more valuable than another. A sea-level restaurant, however, will be a unique amenity. Presently there is no place in Manhattan where a diner can look out at the water instead of down at it. Similarly, the Fulton Fish Market is a unique amenity, even though New Yorkers within sniffing distance may think of it as the opposite. Today's developers realize the market's value and have rejected earlier plans to move it to Brooklyn.

Toronto, Canada: More Than Parks

In Toronto, the Canadian government is transforming a derelict waterfront industrial district into a unique downtown mixed-use development called Harbourfront. Originally, planners proposed to create a grass-and-trees-only waterfront park, but they soon discovered that this single-purpose development was inappropriate. Public policy and needs, financing, and weather dictated a more diverse mixture of activities.

A two-and-a-half mile public promenade on the water's edge with seating and lighting, and several small parks are already in place. There are also restaurants, shops, playgrounds, crafts workshops, a museum, a flea market, historical displays, works of art, an amphitheater, a lagoon, and many other amenities. Still to come are more renovated warehouses with housing, stores, markets, offices, entertainment, and parking facilities.

The government intends now to spend public money—about $27.5 million—to attract an estimated $200 million in private investment. Currently the Canadian government subsidizes the project with about $3 million annually, but by 1987 Harbourfront is expected to be paying its own way.

In return for its investment in public amenities, Toronto expects to generate 600 construction jobs each year and $200 million in income taxes on direct and indirect labor and business earnings during the entire construction period. The Canadian government expects to collect $6 million in indirect revenues.

Reclaiming the Waterfront

The interest in waterfront amenities, planning, and design is a relatively recent phenomenon. Older waterfronts emphasized port, fishing, and industrial activities while amenities were relatively unimportant, but many factors have changed the economy of the waterfront in the past century. Trains, trucks, and airplanes have lessened the importance of water freight. The huge size of today's ocean-going vessels limits them to deep water ports that offer facilities for containerized freight handling and adequate storage for today's huge shipments. New container facilities were often built in a new location, away from old city docks.

Because of the decay and pollution associated with older working waterfronts that have been abandoned by traditional waterfront industries, waterfront land became less valuable in the public's eyes during the period when clean, accessible suburban land seemed unlimited. As a result, some cities simply threw their waterfronts away—they drained them, filled them in, or built super-highways above them.

In the past decade, however, public perception has changed dramatically. We have come to realize that there is less fuel for our cars, that highways are particularly displeasing when they cut through neighborhoods, and that there is only a small amount of developable urban land left. Of this, only a tiny bit is on valuable waterfronts.

Portland, Oregon: Amenities First

Perhaps the best example of what can happen when a community realizes that it is losing access to a treasured waterfront amenity is what happened in Portland, Oregon in the early 1970s. In what has become a classic example of a community rebelling against a highway, the city removed an expressway that had obliterated its waterfront and has begun construction of a park in its place. Construction of the new South Waterfront stage of that park is beginning with a public investment of $16 million to clean up the shore, dredge the marina, build bike paths, and provide street access to downtown Portland. When completed, the marina will have 150 slips for pleasure boats. Though this is 200 less than the

TOM SANDLER, HARBOURFRONT

TOM SANDLER, HARBOURFRONT

number needed, it is all that can be provided on a river still used by working craft. Planners hope that these downtown slips will be used by sailors who moor their boats on the Columbia, ten miles away. With the new marina, people could sail in to have dinner at a downtown Portland restaurant, then sail home again.

Portland officials are not seeking private investment at this stage, for a number of reasons. Larry Dully, Director of Development for the Portland Development Commission, feels that it is important to concentrate on the public amenities at the beginning. The city has public funds in hand and must show public benefits fairly quickly. Since it can proceed with public improvements right away, the city can begin to build a sense of momentum for redevelopment of the site. This makes the area more attractive to developers, who are waiting for the city to carry some of the burden of redevelopment before they invest their funds. Perhaps most important to Portland, an early investment in amenities lets the city control the shape of the development. Once the bike paths, the benches, and the bulkheads are in place, the commercial developments will be limited to areas that the city wants developed.

Portland values this kind of control, because there are ten to 15 people vying for every piece of downtown property available in the city. "Everybody wants to own a piece of downtown Portland," Dully says. Portland is famed as a livable city and has a relatively healthy economy.

Toledo, Ohio: Private Provision of Public Amenities

In a city with greater economic problems, the developer may exert considerably more control over the shape of the waterfront development, but this need not result in poorly constructed waterfront projects. In Toledo, the Owens-Illinois Company is cooperating with the city on the redevelopment of the Maumee River waterfront that provides the company with a handsome and comfortable setting for its headquarters and provides the city with a park full of amenities.

Owens-Illinois felt a commitment to Toledo's revitalization when it built its new headquarters building, but did not want the building in an area that would remain economically distressed. The city and Owens-Illinois agreed to cooperate on a waterfront development on the Maumee River, which flows into Lake Erie. For its part, the city agreed to renovate the existing Promenade Park, behind which the new Owens-Illinois building sits. The city hired the same landscape architecture firm as Owens-Illinois so the two areas would harmonize. Owens-Illinois helped pay for an elevated overlook that connects with the headquarters, included gallery space in the

building's lobby, and provided a pleasure boat harbor, a reflecting pool, skating rink, and public sculpture. The company also helps support the maintenance of the public areas through a trust arrangement with the city.

The local government's role, beyond refurbishing the existing park, is to program events for the public spaces, to provide public transportation, and to landscape the three-block area between the Owens-Illinois facility and the new city-county building. To a certain extent, Owens-Illinois called the shots on this waterfront project, but the citizens of Toledo are the principal beneficiaries.

Economic Benefits of Waterfront Amenities

In both Portland and Toledo, the improved waterfront image will attract people and business, provide jobs and tax revenues, and most importantly, attract commercial development that, in turn, generates more jobs and revenues. The waterfront amenities will also convey a sense of civic spirit, since their presence indicates a community leadership's commitment to the quality of life in the city. Such strong city spirit is very attractive to private investors.

An investor's evaluation of amenities is relatively subjective, compared to the more objective considerations of land and building assembly, market strength, and financial support. Amenities can exercise great influence on investment decisions, but is often difficult to measure.

Traditionally, public funding has paid for parks, promenades, and other public improvements that are attractive to investors. In the past, city officials have tended to offer amenities, along with improvements to roads and utilities, to make a project economically attractive to the developer. This is changing with the current severe economic conditions. Cities with shrinking public resources are now looking for techniques to convince developers to provide the amenities that city wants, but can no longer afford.

When the developer does provide the amenities, as in the case of Toledo's waterfront, the city benefits, but so does the private sector. Benefits can be categorized as direct, indirect, and induced. Direct benefits can usually be measured in dollar and cents: money invested in an amenity, the jobs resulting from it, and the revenue produced by the amenity through user fees, leases, and taxes.

Indirect benefits are those set in motion as a consequence of direct benefits. They tend to multiply, so that they affect the entire economy. Money spent by a waterfront vendor to buy supplies locally is an indirect benefit. Improved productivity by workers who have access to amenities is also an indirect benefit.

One of the first areas to be renovated on the 92 acres of Harbourfront in downtown Toronto was the York Quay Centre, shown at left. The inset shows the site in 1972, derelict and abandoned, before redevelopment. York Quay Centre now houses an art gallery, a theater, a large performance space, a children's play area, and an indoor/outdoor restaurant.

Finally, there are induced benefits, a type of indirect benefit, which may be the most important of all. A person who pays to visit an aquarium is "induced," or lured, there by the promise of exotic sights or the very real pleasure of being near the water.

It is important to understand that an indirect benefit may not be a measurable gain. Money spent to restore an historic ship may be returned in part through entrance fees and mooring leases, but money spent to build a park, open free-of-charge to the public, returns no measurable revenues. If the park makes a positive impact on the image of development and community, and the attitudes and perceptions of those people who decide where a business should relocate, its induced but unmeasurable benefits will usually justify the expense.

There is little statistical information available on the economic aspect of amenities. Even the data that do exist—surveys commissioned by cultural institutions, private developers, and city tourism offices—are often incomplete and potentially misleading. Data are only as good as the method used to measure them, and something as indefinite as benefits from an amenity are difficult to measure concretely.

In survey interviews, active amenities such as festivals, concerts, regattas, and historic ships draw more comment than passive amenities, such as promenades or parks where visitors sit quietly and watch the passing scene, and therefore appear to be more valued. Aquariums, licensed vendors, and marinas can submit their total sales revenues to proclaim their economic success, but this does not mean that amenities that do not produce such revenues are less important.

Economic value does not necessarily correspond with popularity or revenue. Amenities do not exist in a vacuum; they work in a synergistic relationship with other amenities and with commercial and residential development. For example, an annual waterfront festival that is not coordinated with supporting amenities the rest of the year does not create a stable base for the waterfront. A park with grass and trees, but no other amenities, would not attract many people to stop at nearby stores.

The benefits of waterfront development—direct, indirect, and induced—can be considerable. In a paper titled "Urban Waterfront Restoration: The Opportunity, the Benefits, the Need for Support," Peter Epstein list a multitude of reasons why redeveloping a waterfront makes good economic sense.[3] For example, many developments provide new uses for unused industrial and warehouse buildings and bring unused property back into the tax rolls. Open space increases the value of nearby property. As is well known, waterfront development can act as a catalyst for downtown redevelopment. A restored urban waterfront also attracts new tourist income to the community.

Yet another economic benefit is healthier traditional maritime activities, such as commercial fishing, that a restored waterfront can support. Epstein cites a number of other economic benefits of waterfront restoration. The public has better access to a redeveloped waterfront. By redeveloping the waterfront, the city maximizes its investment in water-oriented recreation. A publicly-maintained shoreline helps protect against natural disasters. Waterfront restoration contributes to historic and cultural preservation, and waterfront open spaces encourage economical, compact physical development.

Keys to Success

City officials who perceive the benefits of waterfront amenities are looking to waterfront developments to spark urban revitalization in cities nationwide. When a waterfront works, it works spectacularly well, as demonstrated by the success of the Rouse Company developments. Three factors seem to be vital to this success: the city's commitment to urban revitalization, the development of public amenities, and a viable public-private partnership.

The development of amenities by a city not only benefits the public, but also demonstrates to developers that the city is committed to urban revitalization. According to Scott Ditch, the Rouse Company looks for long-term support from the city government before investing. In Baltimore, he says, what motivated Rouse to invest in the Inner Harbor was the record of the last six mayors, all of whom had enthusiastically supported the waterfront redevelopment and revitalization of downtown Baltimore. Perhaps the most important amenity they had undertaken from the Rouse point of view was the building of a subway; good public transportation matters to a developer who does not want to waste developable land on parking spaces. The City of Baltimore, with its new subway, its strong ethnic neighborhood tradition, its city fair, its nearby office redevelopment, and its plans for cultural facilities around the inner harbor, was an attractive proposition to the Rouse Company.

City officials who hope to follow Baltimore's lead should be warned, however. Many people credit Rouse's Harborplace with turning the tide of urban decay in downtown Baltimore. But Scott Ditch is careful to point out that it was the steps that city officials had already taken toward revitalizing downtown Baltimore—largely the investment in public amenities—that led to Harborplace, not the reverse. The message to city officials is: Don't depend on a private waterfront developer alone to spark revitalization in your city. Get the process started with public amenities so that the developer and the public both know you are in earnest. You will end up with a waterfront that's more profitable for the developer and more livable for the citizens. ◗

Notes:

1. Roger J. Vaughan and Mary Vogel, "Population and Resident Location," in *The Urban Impacts of Federal Policies,* Vol. 4. Santa Monica, California: Rand Corporation, 1979.

2. Much of the recent information on the use of amenities in economic development is collected in a publication of Partners for Livable Places titled "Urban Amenities and Economic Development" (*Livability Digest,* 2(1), Spring 1982). This 80-page digest is available for $5.00 a copy from Partners for Livable Places, 1429 21st Street NW, Washington, DC 20036.

3. Peter Epstein, "Urban Waterfront Restoration: The Opportunity, the Benefits, the Need for Support," in *An Urban Waterfronts Program for California.* Oakland, California: State Coastal Conservancy, 1982.

WEYER PHOTO SERVICE, INC.

In Toledo, Ohio, cooperation between the City and Owens-Illinois Company to redevelop the Maumee River waterfront (above) led to a vital and attractive public recreational center next to the company's new headquarters. In this case, the private sector played a leading role in the development. The City and Owens-Illinois used the same landscape architecture firm to achieve harmony between the public and private elements of the plan.

At left is another view of Baltimore's Harborplace showing one of the historic ships permanently moored. In contrast to the Toledo project, the City of Baltimore took the initiative in the redevelopment, which then led to private investment.

The Urban Edge

Making the Numbers Work: Financing Waterfront Restoration in an Age of Austerity

PETER EPSTEIN

In this final essay we turn to the prosaic but inevitable subject of project economics. Stated crudely: What does a restoration project cost, and who foots the bill? And in somewhat more refined terms: What financial arrangements can be devised that will meet a given project's capital needs and place its long-term operation on a sound financial footing? And how will the various participants, public and private, share in the potential risks and rewards that attend any development venture? Without answers to these questions, the most imaginative of waterfront designs has little chance of being translated into actual brick and mortar—or, to be more "littoral," into rip-rap and pilings.

To date, most successful urban waterfront projects have had as their common denominator the active involvement of the public sector, particularly in underwriting the "front-end" costs of the restoration process. Typical front-end costs include technical studies, land assembly, utilities, and other basic site improvements. Often, these costs must be met before private investors will seriously consider an unproven waterfront location and before the proceeds from permanent, long-term sources of financing are in hand. The rationale for public presence at the front-end is twofold: the unique public interest in the disposition of shorefront property coupled with the equally unique costs and complexities of land development at the water's edge.

Until recently, local sponsors could rely on federal largess to cover much of the high price tag for waterfront restoration. With few exceptions, the recent waterfront successes that have graced the covers of our Sunday supplements—Boston's Quincy Market, Baltimore's Inner Harbor, and Seattle's Pike Street Market—were initiated in the heydey of the federal urban renewal program, which picked up two-thirds of the net costs for land acquisition and basic infrastructure. After Congress shut urban renewal down in 1974, cities could often fill the financing void by packaging funds from a long list of acronymed agencies and programs: OCZM's CEIP, BOR's LWCF, HUD's UDAG and CDBG, and EDA grants, to cite only a few.[1]

The Reagan Administration has moved to terminate or curtail all of these programs. Moreover, the cutbacks are occurring at a time of unprecedented deterioration in the nation's capital markets. High interest rates have truncated the time horizons of all investors, making it particularly difficult to finance long-term, capital-intensive projects such as waterfront restoration.

In today's environment, the financial feasibility of the next Harborplace will depend less on grantsmanship than on the ability of project sponsors to structure new forms of public-private partnership that can mobilize the funds required from private sources of capital. If waterfront designers hope to see their plans move beyond the stage of artists' renderings, the plans themselves must be rooted in an understanding of the special costs inherent in waterfront improvement and the legitimate risk and return requirements of investors.

The Preconditions for Financial Feasibility

Financial plans must provide the documentation and analyses needed to convince a bond underwriter, a lending institution, or a direct equity investor that the venture has been soundly conceived. The heart of any such presentation consists of two elements: a *pro forma* schedule and a capitaliza-

This view of the City of Morro Bay's deteriorated T-pier before its restoration and a sunken fishing boat in Bodega Bay (opposite) dramatize the neglect and physical decay afflicting many waterfronts. The restoration of the T-pier and construction of a new fishing harbor in Bodega Bay were made possible by creative public financing by the State of California, including the State Coastal Conservancy.

tion plan. The *pro forma* details the annual costs and revenues that the sponsor-developer expects as the project is being built and during its initial years of operation. These projections must convince potential investors of the likelihood of a competitive rate of return at acceptable risk and must convince lenders that net income will accrue on a schedule that assures the timely repayment of debt. Similarly, the capitalization plan must demonstrate realistic prospects for raising the combination of equity, working capital, construction, and permanent financing required to carry out the project.

The requirements for achieving financial credibility can best be understood by first examining the cost and revenue sides of development on the waterfront.

The Cost Premium on Waterfront Restoration

Building at the water's edge is costly when compared with other publicly-sponsored efforts to redevelop urban land. Here are a few reasons why:

- Land assembly on the waterfront can prove beyond the capability of any private developer, due to title problems, fragmented ownership, and illogical lot lines. These problems, many attributable to the age of waterfront districts, may be further complicated by issues of riparian rights, tidelands grants, and the overlay of utility and railroad easements. Highly fragmented land ownership is also common to many "newer" waterfront communities laid out by real estate speculators in the early 1900s, prior to the existence of any local planning or effective land use controls.

- The age of waterfront districts also means that basic municipal infrastructure may be obsolete and deteriorated and that street patterns are cramped and anachronistic.

- Shoreline protection requires special expenditures to replace rotted pier decks and pilings, to replenish sand beaches and stabilize dunes, and to install or rebuild rip-rap, bulkheads, seawalls, jetties, and breakwaters.

- Traditional maritime activities such as commercial fishing lend color and an authentic robustness to waterfront life. In well-conceived restoration plans, these activities can continue to flourish and complement—rather than compete with—newer types of tourist-oriented uses. However, upgrading a harbor to support a competitive fishing industry can prove particularly costly. Old channels may have silted in; new or deeper channels may have to be dredged; wharves may have

deteriorated beyond repair; storage, boat repair, processing, and distribution facilities may all be antiquated. Modernization may require investment in high-speed unloading equipment, pneumatic ice plants, high-pressure washer and pumpout systems, cold storage marketing facilities, and marine elevators.

- Marina development is often viewed as an essential "loss leader" in the financial program for commercial waterfront development—both to draw visitors who will patronize restaurants and shops, and to enhance the value of shorefront properties for residential development.[2] A typical small craft harbor costs from about $5,000 to $20,000 per berth, depending on the amount of dredging, diking, and breakwater construction required.

- The natural hazards of a shoreline location can also add to costs; development must be protected against floods and gales as well as the more insidious effects of exposure over time to sea fog and salt water.

- Many prime waterfront sites consist of filled land, often of recent vintage. Building on these unstable soils may require piling or deep foundations. For example, on the east shore of San Francisco Bay, piling requirements typically add up to $10 per square foot to building costs. Closing down a sanitary landfill can involve costly measures to dike and seal the fill in order to prevent pollutants from seeping into adjacent waters.

- Pollution-free waters are a prerequisite for making full use of the waterfront amenity. Adequate systems to treat sewage effluent and to divert storm runoff often involve capital expenses of intimidating proportions.

- This book has underscored the importance of public access and open space as a critical ingredient of beneficial waterfront restoration. Escalating land prices can grossly inflate land assembly costs for these purposes—particularly where private real estate speculators have already recognized the potential for shoreline redevelopment and local government is acting after the fact to include provision for public uses. In California, urban land prices for properties fronting on bay or sea range from as low as $3 per square foot (or about $125,000 per acre) in the depressed mill towns of the north coast to as high as $250 per square foot in the more affluent residential enclaves of southern California. Moreover, the development of public shoreline accessways may

The restoration of San Francisco's Fort Mason complex is one of the most innovative public waterfront re-use efforts. Part of the Golden Gate National Recreation Area, Fort Mason hosts an amazing variety of cultural, educational, recreational, and public service organizations in facilities once used as a major troop embarkation point during World War II.

require public expenditures to undo or to work around the planning mistakes of the past—for example, to reroute a highway that preempts the shoreline, or to construct platforms or bridges over highway or rail corridors which cannot be discontinued.

- Because of the special public concern over coastal land and navigable waterways, waterfront development typically involves time-consuming and costly delays to secure numerous permit approvals. Many of these approvals are in addition to those required under standard land use and building regulation. In California, depending on the nature and location of the project, permits may have to be obtained from the U.S. Army Corps of Engineers, the California Coastal Commission, the Department of the Interior, the federal Environmental Protection Agency, the California Departments of Fish and Game and of Boating and Waterways, the State Water Resources Control Board, the State Lands Commission, and regional bodies such as the Bay Area Conservation and Development Commission (BCDC) which regulates fill activity in San Francisco Bay.

All these expenses are in addition to those common to any urban development project which strives to achieve a high quality of urban design, provide special amenities, and recycle deteriorated buildings to new uses.

The Upside Potential

In light of the bleak prospects for major federal grants, where will the money come from to pay the high price tag of waterfront revival? More than ever before, project feasibility will hinge upon including sufficient income-generating uses to make the development as self-supporting as possible. This in turn may depend on a demonstration that, although waterfront development involves unique costs, it also can generate uniquely high revenues and profits.

The previous essay in this volume has argued that amenities pay—above all by drawing visitors (i.e., customers) to waterfront districts and enhancing property values. These arguments apply directly to the income or revenue side of the economic equation. Increased patronage means higher rates per square foot of retail space, a more rapid turnover of restaurant seats, higher room and occupancy rates for hotels. All of these translate into higher gross receipts per unit of commercial space. Similarly, property value means strong demand—and prices—for residential units, more secure collateral for mortgage loans, and increased property tax receipts to repay any public borrowings.

The pioneering risks taken by James Rouse and other entrepreneurs have already demonstrated the "upside potential" of well conceived, mixed-use development in a waterfront location. In the developer's parlance, "upside potential" means the return to the investor if a completed project performs in

accordance with the most optimistic projections. For example, both the Quincy Market development in Boston and Harborplace in Baltimore involved a substantial gamble that the architecture and activities would draw the customers required to turn a profit. In the end, they did that and more. As the publicists love to note—applying the contemporary standard of turnstile success—both projects have been attracting more visitors per year than Disney World. These successes should make it easier for other waterfront developers, public and private, to convince the financial community that the income is there to recover the high costs of building at the water's edge. The success of Baltimore's waterfront revival is particularly heartening since—in contrast to Boston's—it was accomplished solely on the basis of overall design and programming, without the headstart of an existing tourist base and an inventory of important historical structures. This does not mean that every ocean and riverfront community can expect to duplicate the success of Harborplace. Optimism must be tempered by the realities of each local market.

Risk Allocation: The Key to a Workable Financial Structure

The plans for restoring any given stretch of urban shoreline may conjure up visions of bustling promenades, crowded bistros and chowder houses, dry docks, chandleries, picturesque armadas of fishing trawlers and pleasure craft, laughter, gaiety, sunlight—and, wafted to and fro on the sea breeze, the ineffable music of ringing cash registers. Yet, no matter how compelling the vision, the project sponsor still confronts an uphill struggle to assemble the financing required to give it life.

The key to a workable financial and organizational structure for any urban development venture is careful attention to analysis and allocation of financial risks. By its nature, development work involves uncertainties like construction scheduling, local approvals, inflation, future interest rates, manage-

ment capability to control costs, market demand, regulatory changes (e.g., future IRS rulings), resale values and liquidity, and acts of God. The major task that confronts the project sponsor is how best to allocate these risks among all the participants—contractors, primary lenders, active and passive investors, secondary market institutions, lawyers, property owners, private mortgage insurers, various levels of government, other insuring entities, and, ultimately, the purchasers and tenants of the restored properties.

In particular, there are two major tactics a public agency can adopt in its efforts to assemble a financial structure attractive to private investors.

- The public agency can help shelter the private investor from serious financial exposure until the project is planned, built, and operating successfully.

- The public agency can organize the undertaking to maximize the federal tax benefits available to private participants.

In most situations, a private developer's chief concern will be to minimize the amount of equity capital he has at risk in a project before it has established its market and begun to generate a net operating income. Even after a complex is built, it may take some time for space to be leased and businesses to become profitable. A key to securing developer commitment may be the public agency's willingness to assume the initial risks of holding the land and making site improvements until the completed project is up and running.[3] In exchange, however, the agency should be able to negotiate important concessions—perhaps even some direct participation in the venture's upside profitability. For example, the City of Norwich, Connecticut will receive a share in the profits of condominium construction on a riverfront site as the quid pro quo for its constructing a bulkhead and making the parcel available.

San Francisco's historic cable cars terminate at the Hyde Street Pier and the Cannery, two major tourist attractions created by public and private restoration efforts. The Pier is a state park, while the Cannery houses a variety of commercial enterprises. The National Park Service now operates tours to Alcatraz Island, seen in the background, once a federal penitentiary.

BRUCE KLIEWE / JEROBOAM, INC.

Creative Tax Planning

Local governments can also make projects inviting to private investors by structuring public-private involvement so that private participants can take maximum advantage of the tax benefits available to real estate investors—investment credits, depreciation allowances, interest deductions, and tax deferral through installment purchase contracts. The price that a developer can pay for a ground lease, development rights, or purchase of land itself is limited to the residual that remains after projecting his income from rents or sales, deducting the costs of construction, management, taxes, and debt service, and allowing for his targeted rate of return. Thus, to the extent that a public-private joint venture is structured to increase the tax benefits for private participants, the public sponsor can command a higher price for making a usable site available to the developer.

Even where the intended land uses may be purely public, opportunities for private participation still exist. For example, consider a plan to convert a dilapidated warehouse into a maritime museum. Normally, in the absence of grants or philanthropic donations, the public sponsor would simply carry out the conversion with funds either appropriated from the local treasury or borrowed privately. However, it may prove advantageous for the public sponsor to sell the structure to a private investor, who can take advantage of the unusually generous tax write-offs for rehabilitating historic buildings, and then lease the finished space back for the museum. Thanks to the private investor's tax savings, the lease payments he requires for his investment to be profitable may well be less than the annual debt payments that the public agency would otherwise owe if it had retained ownership of the remodeled building.

Leased Revenue Bonds

This essay has underscored the importance of a public agency assuming the burden of "front-end" costs as a precondition for attracting private investment. Of course, this assumes that the agency has the ability to finance these costs—if not from grants or reserves in the city treasury, then with borrowed funds.

Where money must be borrowed, the preferred financing technique is to issue some form of tax exempt revenue bond financing. A revenue bond pledges a specific revenue source to repay the debt. The tax exemption on the interest paid to the lender makes capital available to the project at low interest rates. Revenue bond financing has the further attraction of insulating the local government from liability for repayment—in contrast to so-called general obligation bonds, commonly used to finance school construction and other public works, which pledge the entire resources of the city treasury to guarantee the debt.

Two specific bonding concepts with applicability to waterfront restoration are "lease revenue bonds" and "tax allocation bonds." Where a city or port authority or other public sponsor owns a prime waterfront site, development can be carried out under various types of lease arrangements, with the public retaining ownership of the underlying property. The projected stream of future payments from leases can then be used to secure the tax-exempt revenue bond.

Leasehold arrangements can be structured in many ways. Sometimes, the public sponsor will make all or most of the property available to a developer under some form of master ground lease. As master lessee, the developer will then construct new buildings and/or renovate existing structures, market the space to other users, provide ongoing management for the income-producing properties, and perhaps assume responsibility for neighboring public areas as well.

Alternatively, the public sponsor can essentially subdivide the property and negotiate the separate ground leases for each parcel. Or, more ambitiously, it can assume the developer role by constructing and renovating facilities and then leasing out building space rather than just the underlying ground or pier.

The master ground lease option has several virtues from the public agency perspective: it ensures that development of the entire property will proceed according to a unified design; the agency has to deal with only one lessee rather than many; and a master lease places the entrepreneurial and management headaches on the lessee. Moreover, when a ground lease is involved, the private lessee has a greater stake in the project than if he rents finished building space since his own capital is invested in the facilities constructed on the leasehold.

On the other hand, a number of public agencies have preferred to assume the full entrepreneurial role themselves in order to retain more direct control over design, construction, and management. Lease terms usually involve some combination of cash payment, rent, and a percentage of gross revenues.

For the public agency, the financial feasibility of a waterfront project may depend on the ability to recover public investment costs from the projected lease revenues. For example, a large (8,000 square foot) and successful waterfront restaurant might gross $2 million annually (or $250 per square foot). At three percent of gross revenues, a ground lease would provide the public sponsor with $60,000. This would support the debt service on $450,000 of revenue bonds, assuming an interest rate of ten percent over twenty years.[4]

Tax Allocation Bonds

California communities have pioneered another bond technique called the tax allocation or tax increment bond. Under this approach, the repayment of a revenue bond is secured by a pledge of the increased property tax revenues that will accrue from successful redevelopment. This makes tax allocation bonds a particularly potent financing technique in waterfront projects because of the tremendous land value creation. For example, in the mid-1960s, the City of Ventura, California converted a blighted expanse of beachfront property into a waterfront promenade and a small park, with a hotel and new housing. Prior to the project, the real estate involved was valued at only $165,000 for tax purposes; today, its assessed value exceeds $3 million. The projected tax increment in the waterfront district was used to float about $2 million in bonds.[5]

The tax allocation district may be strictly limited to the parcels on which improvements will be planned, or it may also encompass neighboring areas, where property values and assessed valuations will presumably rise.

The passage of Proposition 13, which imposed tight ceilings on property tax rates and assessments in California, has lessened the potency of tax allocation bonding as a financing technique. Nonetheless, it remains a useful tool here and certainly has great untapped potential in states without such property tax limitations.

Earmarked Revenue Sources

Another funding strategy is to identify certain revenue sources that have some logical connection to waterfront activities and to use these funds for restoration purposes. This was probably one of the rationales behind the federal Coastal Energy Impact Program, which linked capital grants and loans to coastal communities to the amount of off-shore leasing for oil drilling purposes.

At the local level, city governments often allocate a portion of the tax on hotel and motel rooms to activities that promise to generate more tourist activity and increase the demand for overnight lodging. Other local revenue sources that can be linked to waterfront improvement include taxes and fees collected on marina facilities and pleasure craft.

Transferable Development Credits

In some instances, innovative regulatory approaches can substitute for the direct public investment that would otherwise be required to achieve waterfront restoration objectives. One such concept is the Transferable Development Credit (TDC). TDCs are a mechanism for compensating property owners for restrictions on the use of their land without the expenditure of public funds to provide the compensation.

The underlying concept is a simple one. Assume, for example, a waterfront parcel occupied by an early nineteenth century mercantile building in danger of being replaced by a high-rise office structure. In exchange for preserving the historic structure, the property owner receives development rights or credits. A development credit is the right to build a specified amount of space—one residential unit, for example, or 1,000 square feet of office space. These development credits can then be "transfered" to other "receiver sites" identified as suitable for more intensive development. The property owner can use the credits or sell them to another party.

Where a large number of donor and receiver parcels are involved, the objective is to create a self-regulating private market in TDCs. In some cases, however, a public agency may have to act as a banker of TDCs—the buyer and seller of last resort—in order to prime the market mechanism.

To date, about twenty-five towns, counties, and regional governments have experimented with variations on the TDC concept. In most cases, the objective has been to preserve farmland or other scenic areas subject to development pressures. For example, the California State Coastal Conservancy is overseeing TDC programs in the Santa Monica Mountains and in Big Sur. But the TDC concept has also been used to save urban landmark buildings, including the Fulton Fish Market in the historic South Street Seaport district of New York City.

Incentive Zoning

Incentive zoning is another regulatory concept with applicability to waterfront development. Under incentive zoning, a private developer is permitted an increase in the density of use that would normally be permitted under conventional zoning and subdivision controls—for example, an increased height limit or more housing units per acre. In exchange for this density bonus, the developer agrees to provide some desired amenity or public benefit.

In the context of urban waterfront restoration, a developer might agree to contribute public open space and facilities, preserve a facade or other architectural features, dedicate a right-of-way to the water's edge, commission artworks for public spaces, pick up the costs of repairing public piers or embankments, contribute to a maintenance fund for public spaces, or submit plans to a rigorous design review. Or the density bonus can be conditioned on an agreement to incorporate specific architectural features into the developer's building to integrate it into a unified urban design plan for the entire waterfront district.

California's many public recreational piers, such as the Manhattan Beach Pier shown opposite, are heavily used by both residents and visitors. Amenities like these piers are valuable complements to commercial waterfront development, and indirectly contribute to the total economic health of their communities.

The benefit to be provided can be determined either on a formula basis or through a case-by-case negotiation. In its more sophisticated applications, the incentive zoning process attempts to equate the cost of the concession by developer with the capitalized value of the increased density allowance. By its nature, incentive zoning is most applicable to waterfront planning where a local agency seeks to concentrate high density uses on one portion of the shoreline in order to relieve development pressures on the remainder.

A Call for Public Entrepreneurship

The economic obstacles to realizing waterfront plans loom up ahead—intimidating, but not insurmountable—even in these days of stingy federal budgets and high prime rates. The cement mixers and cranes on sites at Norfolk, Virginia; Manhattan's South Street Seaport; Monterey, California; and Seattle's Central Waterfront are evidence of the continued bankability of well-conceived projects. Moreover, thanks to the spectacular profitability of the carnivals of commerce orchestrated by the Rouse firm in Boston and Baltimore, an aura of success now surrounds the general concept of waterfront restoration. This should help new projects overcome the inherent skepticism of the financial community. And a number of approaches for melding public and private interests in the reuse of the water's edge have been tested and await more widespread application. The ideas and opportunities are there, but the times require a special brand of public entrepreneurship if the momentum of waterfront revival is to be sustained. Entrepreneurship in this context means the imagination and financial savvy to structure attractive incentives for private invest-

ment, the negotiating skills to ensure that the terms for securing such investment do not compromise the community's long-term interest in the quality of waterfront design and in opening the shoreline for the enjoyment of everyone, and, above all else, the energy to make things happen. ●

Notes:

1. To translate: the Office of Coastal Zone Management's Coastal Energy Impact Program, the Bureau of Outdoor Recreation's Land and Water Conservation Fund, the Department of Housing and Urban Development's Urban Development Action Grants and Community Development Block Grants, and the Economic Development Agency's Public Works Grants. Over the years, the U.S. Army Corps of Engineers has contributed dredging and other harbor improvements to numerous local waterfront projects.

2. From a public policy perspective, subsidy of marinas is often questionable, particularly where marina construction will cause ecological damage and the benefits will accrue primarily to the privileged few who own yachts.

3. Even when the public sponsor assumes virtually all the up-front risk, it will still want to insist on enough of a private financial investment to ensure that any private developer has a financial stake in meeting his commitments. This financial stake can take the form of option payments, an initial installment payment on the site, or a performance bond.

4. This calculation assumes that the bondholders require that projected annual revenues exceed annual debt payments on the bond by at least twenty-five percent. In practice, revenue bonds are rarely issued for amounts of less than one million dollars; lease revenue from several commercial facilities would be combined to repay the bonds.

5. In California, a "possessory interest" tax is paid on the value of all improvements made by private lessees on publicly owned land. Thus the tax allocation bond remains a financing option even when the underlying land remains in public ownership.

"Do no dishonour to the earth lest you dishonour the spirit of man."
— Henry Beston[1]

Conclusion

We began with the premise that design for the coastal edge requires a special sensitivity. An historical review of design on the California coast and a review of existing conditions in coastal towns has shown that this has not always been present. Descriptions of successful publicly sponsored projects have shown that state and local governments can promote excellence in coastal design. And finally, discussions of the economics of waterfront restoration have shown that environmentally sound design can be economically sound as well.

There is room for diverse interests on the waterfront and the entire coastal edge. The need for multiple uses can be accommodated in many ways; there are many designs that meet the Coastal Act's requirements. The public sector—state and local government—has a basic responsibility to foster the best and most appropriate use of the waterfront and the coast. Design professionals and their clients, as creators of structures which will dot the coastal landscape for years to come, are obligated to work within publicly established constraints. And of course, the ultimate responsibility for preservation of the coastal edge belongs to the public. A policy and regulatory framework—like the California Coastal Act—can establish the boundaries within which multiple uses of waterfront land can be accommodated. Operating within these boundaries, public agencies can use the creative development approach to resolve coastal land use and design conflicts. In this way, public enjoyment and use of the coast can be achieved; sensitive coastal resources can be protected; and legitimate private investment can be made in a manner consistent with environmentally sound policies and regulations.

Notes:

1. Henry Beston, *The Outermost House* (New York: The Viking Press, 1956), p. 222.

About the authors

WILLIAM M. BOYD is currently a staff attorney for the Irvine Company and was formerly on the staff of the State Coastal Conservancy and Chief Counsel for the California Coastal Commission. His experience includes private practice as well as public law. He was one of the principal drafters of the 1976 Coastal Act, including the local planning provisions and many of the policy sections. He has studied urban and regional planning in Brazil and Mediterranean coastal planning under Ford and Fulbright grants, and has lectured extensively in land use law and coastal management for organizations such as the American Bar Association and the California Continuing Education of the Bar.

PETER S. BRAND was project manager for the State Coastal Conservancy's initial experiments in community participation and design. At the Conservancy, he has organized urban waterfront projects with a special emphasis on the interaction of design and planning professionals with the community. He was responsible for the initial organization of this book.

GRAY BRECHIN is currently design critic for KRON-TV. As an architectural historian for the Foundation for San Francisco's Architectural Heritage, he has consulted on easement evaluation, EIR criticism, and decisions regarding threatened buildings. Brechin has been very active in bringing public attention to the architectural history of San Francisco, through public and media appearances. His publications include numerous articles on architectural, social, and natural history for the *California Monthly, Daily Californian, Berkeley Gazette, California Living, Sierra,* and *Defenders of Wildlife.*

JIM BURNS is a consultant to professional, public, and community organizations interested in community participation in design and planning projects. He has worked on five major coastal community participation projects in California, as well as in many other communities throughout the United States. Formerly the Senior Editor of *Progressive Architecture,* he is author of *Connections: Ways to Discover and Realize Community Potentials* and (with Lawrence Halprin) *Taking Part: A Workshop Approach to Collective Creativity.*

PETER EPSTEIN has consulted for over fifteen years on urban development activities with clients from all levels of government and the private sector. He contributed to *An Urban Waterfronts Program for California,* a Coastal Conservancy report to the California Legislature. He has served as director of the Massachusetts Office of Local Development, which provides financial and technical assistance to local urban waterfront projects.

DAVID GEBHARD, an architectural historian, teaches at the University of California, Santa Barbara; is Vice Chairman of the Landmark Committee, City of Santa Barbara, and is past President of the Society of Architectural Historians. He has authored or co-authored a number of volumes on California architecture and planning including *L.A. in the Thirties, R.M. Schindler, California, 1878–1908, A Guide to Architecture in San Francisco and Northern California,* and *A Guide to Architecture in Los Angeles and Southern California.*

PETER GRENELL is currently a development consultant and was formerly the Assistant to the Executive Officer of the State Coastal Conservancy, and Acting Executive Officer in the Executive Officer's absence. As such, he managed and organized programs related to urban waterfront restoration, coastal access, agricultural preservation, and housing. He initiated the Conservancy's Access Program, and assisted in the legislative passage of the California Urban Waterfront Area Restoration Financing Authority (CUWARFA) Act of 1983. He has worked as a planning consultant both in the United States and overseas, serving as a regional planner for the Ford Foundation in Calcutta, India, as a program officer for the United Nations' Children's Fund (UNICEF) in India, and as urban development consultant to the Corporacion Venezolana de Guayana for construction of Ciudad Guayana in Venzuela. He also toured the urban waterfronts of Europe as part of a study program sponsored by the German Marshall Fund of the United States and the Institute for European Environmental Policy.

PATRICIA A. HUNTER is a Senior Associate for Open Space Management at Partners for Livable Places, and has been a practicing landscape architect specializing in urban design and open space management strategies in both the public and private sectors.

ROBERT H. McNULTY is the president of Partners for Livable Places, a nonprofit coalition of organizations and individuals dedicated to improving the quality of life in our nation's communities. McNulty is a nationally known authority in the field of urban conservation and related patterns of private/public sector cooperation. Prior to founding Partners, he was Assistant Director of the Architecture/Environment Arts Program of the National Endowment for the Arts.

CHARLES W. MOORE, F.A.I.A., an internationally known architect, earned his Ph.D. from Princeton University in 1957 with a dissertation on the role of water in architecture. Several of his most notable design projects have been located on the world's edges—such as Condominium I in Sea Ranch, a coastal development noted for ecologically sound architecture. Currently, Moore is a principal in the firm of Moore, Ruble, and Yudell in Los Angeles; the firm has completed several major planning and design projects for communities on the California coast.

JOSEPH E. PETRILLO is the Executive Officer of the State Coastal Conservancy. Prior to his appointment, he was a consultant to the California Senate Select Committee on Land Use Management and played the major role in drafting the California Coastal Act of 1976. As Staff Counsel to the California Coastal Commission, he directed the permit appeals program and drafted the sections of the California Coastal Plan that developed the financial, organizational, and legal basis of California's coastal resources protection program.

SALLY WOODBRIDGE, architectural historian, has co-authored a number of books on architecture, including *Buildings of the Bay Area, A Guide to Architecture in San Francisco and Northern California, Bay Area Houses, A Guide to the Architecture of the State of Washington,* and the *Historic American Buildings Survey Catalogue for California.* She has worked as a consultant in the evaluation of historic sites, has taught numerous courses on architectural history, and has served as West Coast Corresponding Editor for *Progressive Architecture.*

INDEX

INDEX